C000176688

ALL THE KING'S COOKS

ALL THE KING'S COOKS

THE TUDOR KITCHENS OF KING HENRY VIII AT HAMPTON COURT PALACE

PETER BREARS

SOUVENIR PRESS

First published in 1999 by
Souvenir Press Ltd.,
43 Great Russell Street, London WC1B 3PA

ISBN 0 285 63533 6

Printed in Singapore

Contents

Introduction

Henry VIII was one of the most remarkable of monarchs, a man of great mental and physical energy, whose dynamic policies revolutionised the social and political life of the whole country. The most prolific of all royal builders, he created a series of magnificent palaces, the greatest capable of housing and feeding his entire court, including hundreds of nobles, courtiers, officers of state, guards, and a virtual army of household servants. The efficient organisation of an entourage of this scale and complexity, making sure that all the expected services were delivered promptly and with the minimum of wastage and loss, was a practical and administrative problem of the greatest magnitude. But by adapting and reforming centuries of accumulated experience, Henry VIII's officers and the workers they controlled were able to ensure that the Tudor court functioned remarkably smoothly.

A great variety of sources, such as household regulations, accounts, menus and recipes, still remain to help us to elucidate the everyday life of the court, but among the most important, and certainly the most evocative, are the actual buildings where these activities took place. Over the course of time, many of them have been demolished or rebuilt, but Hampton Court, and particularly the kitchens there, survive in a remarkable and truly unique state of completeness.

Hampton Court Palace, with its six acres of buildings, is one of the largest and most remarkable of all our historic properties. Extended by Cardinal Wolsey from 1514 and Henry VIII from 1525, and again by William and Mary in the late seventeenth century, it had been abandoned as a royal residence by the 1750s. From that time, its great state apartments were rarely visited, and much of the remaining accommodation was divided up into grace-and-favour residences. In the 1830s this unusually quiet interlude ended when William IV began to restore and refurbish the interiors for the ever-growing number of ordinary visitors who now came down for the day from London. When Queen Victoria reopened the state apartments in November 1838 the crowds flooded in, 350,000 visiting in the year of the Great Exhibition alone. Since that time the palace has, with minor exceptions, remained open to the public. And it has continued to attract numerous visitors from throughout the world, especially since the early

1990s following the restoration of the state apartments after the disastrous fire and the opening of many new facilities.

The popularity of Hampton Court is easily explained. It has something to interest everyone. Set behind the grandeur of its formal gardens and the wonderful Tudor and Wren façades lie interiors of the highest quality, furnished with the Royal Collection of tapestries, paintings and furniture, all of bewildering richness and intricate detail. However many times you visit, there is always more to see and more to learn about its creation and function over the centuries, as well as about those who have lived there. Many fine books have been written on its history, of which Ernest Law's *The History of Hampton Court Palace in Tudor Times* (1885) perhaps remains the most comprehensive. Those published in recent years have demonstrated the highest standards of scholarship; the works of Dr Simon Thurley, the first Curator of the Historic Royal Palaces agency, are exemplary in this field. By combining a wealth of meticulous documentary research with masses of archaeological and other detailed evidence, he has thrown a fascinating light on the development and function of Hampton Court's state apartments, its formal gardens and its service wings. In addition, his supervising of the display of the palace's Tudor kitchens ready for their reopening in 1991 was marked by an admirable flair.

Given the already existing wealth of books on the subject, the need for yet another on the Hampton Court kitchens may well be questioned. But perhaps my rather different approach will justify this volume, and it may be best explained by an account of my experience of putting the kitchens back into practical operation.

I had already provided minor details of information for the refurbishment of the kitchens, as well as modelling the sugar sculptures for the displays, and it was on the strength of this that the marketing division of Historic Royal Palaces, the body which operates Hampton Court Palace, asked me – at fairly short notice – to put on a public demonstration of the kitchens in use, as they would have been in the 1530s and '40s. This was a formidable challenge, particularly since it would be the first historic re-enactment to be arranged in any of the royal palaces, and therefore the fate of similar future events would depend upon its success. Numerous practical problems, such as the protection of the historic surfaces from the heat and spillage which always attend practical cookery, had to be overcome, but with the invaluable cooperation of the palace's housekeeper effective solutions were worked out. Together with my colleagues Marc Meltonville, Gary Smedley and Adrian Warrell I was able to provide most of the accurate reproductions of costume, cooking equipment and tableware, and the palace generously allowed us to use its new reproduction spits for roasting meats before the great open log fire. Because of the palace's long opening hours there was no opportunity for a trial run, but we felt that every eventuality that could reasonably be anticipated had been accommodated by the evening of Boxing Day, 1991, when we moved into our rooms in the original confectionary, just twelve hours before the demonstration was due to open to the public.

Next morning, just after eight o'clock, we went down to the Tudor kitchens and started to set up our work-tables, to clad the stewing stoves with firebrick and sheet steel, fill the charcoal bunkers, and unpack and arrange all the chafing dishes, bowls, cooking pots and the numerous other items of equipment that we had brought with us.

Moving into any strange kitchen always presents challenges – but here both the time scale and the pressure were exceptional, for within fifteen minutes the butcher arrived with the roast of the day, a huge pig, over five feet from tail to snout, appropriate to the importance of the occasion. The butcher was immediately followed by the press, comprising several national and regional television and radio crews, and dozens of reporters and photographers representing newspapers, magazines and agencies. Clearly, it was a great visual news story. This was the first time since the 1740s that anyone had cooked in Wolsey's great kitchen, and now cooks in authentically styled clothes were to demonstrate how it was actually carried out – for real!

As the cameras whirred and flashed, the pig was laid out along the table, its mouth already held open by a wooden wedge. It was only at this point, as one of the spits was being passed to me, that I realised that we had a real problem: the spit, commissioned by a purely academic historian, was so flimsy that the weight of a mere chicken, I suspected, would make it flex. So we pushed the spit through the length of the pig, and tried its strength by lifting it at both ends. The result of this experiment had been too predictable – the spit's ends were now bowing upwards from the extremities of the dead weight of the carcase, which our joint effort had failed to shift by so much as a millimetre. Fortunately, though, after straightening the spit, inserting another two alongside it and then rapidly binding them together with stout iron wire, we were finally able to raise the pig, place it on the huge cob-irons in front of the fire, and rotate it before the fierce heat of the flaming logs. This whole process took no more than a few minutes, and produced enough photographs and articles to ensure that the palace's Tudor kitchen project enjoyed nationwide publicity. This success was entirely due to the presence of mind and sleight-of-hand of the cooks, without whose expertise the palace's attempt at reproducing this most essential piece of Tudor kitchen equipment would have turned a memorable press call into a public humiliation, and a great public event into a shambles.

1. *The Kitchens, Hampton Court* Here the kitchens are seen from the north, as shown in Anthonis van der Wyngaerde's watercolour drawing of around 1558 on which the top drawing is based. The key is numbered from right to left, following the progress of the food from the Outer Court through to the Great Hall.

1. Outer Court
2. Great House of Ease (latrines)
3. Back Gate
4. Porters' Lodge (?)
5. Yeoman and groom of the Counting House (?)
6. Jewel House
7,8. Comptroller's lodgings
9. Comptroller's Cellar
10. King's Coal House
11. Greencloth Yard
12. Spicery office
13. Chandlery
14. Moat
15. Clerk comptroller
16. Inner gateway
17. Bottle House (Salt Beef Store?)
18. Dry Fish House
19. Pastry Yard
20. Scullery office
21. Pastry office
22. Confectionary
23. Pastry Bakehouse
24. Pastry workhouse
25. Pastry (Storehouse? Boulting House?)

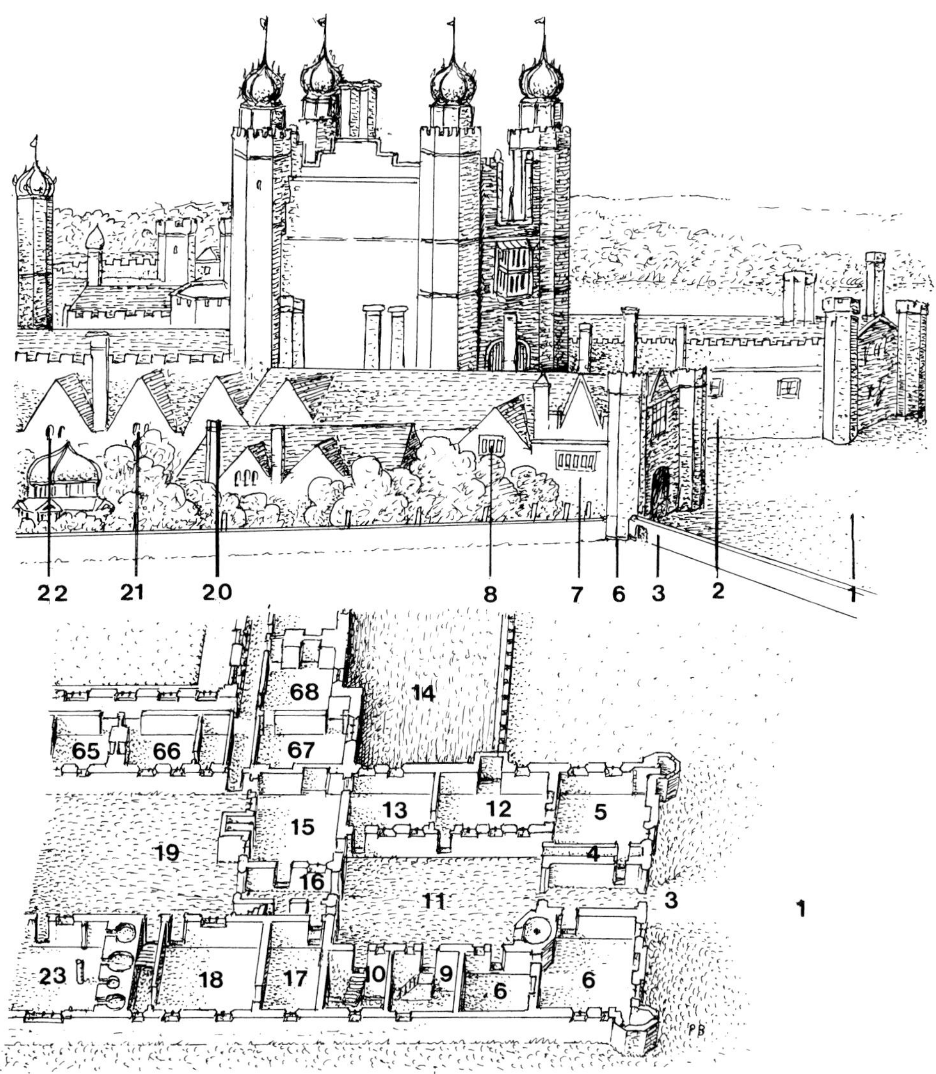

26. Boiling House
27. Paved Passage (Fish Court)
28. Dry Larder
29. Stair from Buttery to Great Hall
30–31. Hall-place workhouses
32. Wet Larder
33. Larder
34. Hall-place dresser office
35. Hall-place dresser
36. Pewter Scullery
37. Scullery Yard
38. Cooks' lodgings (?)
39. Hall-place kitchen
40. Great Hall
41. Lord's-side kitchen
42. Lord's-side dresser office
43. Silver Scullery (?)
44. The Great Space
45. Lord's-side kitchen-work-house
46. Clerk of the kitchen's lodgings
47. Wafery and lodgings for surgeons and others
48. Stairs to Great Watching Chamber
49. Drinking House
50. Great Wine Cellar
51. Privy Wine Cellar
52. Stairs to Great Watching Chamber
53. Beer Cellar
54. Stairs to Great Hall
55. Almonry
56. Bread delivery room
57. Privy Buttery
58. Great Buttery
59. Base Court
60–68. Lodgings

Unless documentary research is complemented by real practical knowledge, our view of the past can be dangerously distorted!

Even before the press had departed, the public began to arrive in droves. It was clear from the start that they found this new way of understanding the life of the palace exciting – seeing everything actually happening around them far surpassed the experience offered by even the best guidebooks and sound-guides. Not only that, but they could ask questions, talk about what was going on, and pass on their own observations and information to us cooks. To encourage this, we remained our own 1990s selves rather than adopting Tudor pronunciation, grammar and personalities. To the numerous overseas visitors anything but modern English would anyway have been incomprehensible. Our purpose was to encourage an understanding of the palace kitchens, their buildings, features, organisation and practical operation.

Throughout the day, people kept returning to the kitchens to see the roasting, boiling, frying and so forth, as the various dishes were prepared. Then, at three in the afternoon, an appropriate time for a Tudor midwinter supper, we cleared the great working table, set it as if for dining in the Great Hall, and gave a talk and demonstration on Tudor food and table manners to over three hundred people who had managed to pack themselves into the room. Perhaps having only seen Tudor table manners as demonstrated by Charles Laughton in the 1933 film *The Private Life of Henry VIII* – wrenching a drumstick off a roast fowl, tearing off a gross mouthful and then tossing the bone over his shoulder – or perhaps having attended one of those 'medieval banquets' beloved of popular caterers, they were amazed and intrigued to see how easy it was to dine cleanly and elegantly using just a knife, a spoon and the fingers.

Over the course of the next few days, thousands of visitors passed through the kitchens, all enthusing about what they were experiencing and asking a never-ending stream of questions, most of which were effectively answered. By the end of the last day we were totally exhausted, having cooked and talked non-stop for over seven hours each day in the freezing cold, not to mention the five hours of preparation, washing up and cleaning. All this was well worth the effort, though, for the whole event had proved an outstanding success, in terms of visitor numbers and income, as well as our visitors' evident enjoyment.

Since then, we have organised a similar event between 27 December and New Year's Day each year for the palace's marketing division. They have allowed us to expand both the number of cooks and the range of activities, so that each successive year has seen improvements in the quality and content of the demonstrations. It has been a mutually beneficial experience. The palace has gained a very popular and profitable seasonal event, while the visitors have gained many outstanding and memorable experiences – as they describe in the books left out for their comments: 'This is the way to teach social history. Thank you for an extremely interesting and most enjoyable tour.' . . . 'Superb in every way and so clearly explained by your dedicated and expert staff.' . . . 'Wonderful to explore a real kitchen with such enthusiastic guides and a real commitment to history.' . . . 'The real way to learn about the past is to see it "live" in this way. Fantastic for the children and adults.' . . . From a personal point of view, I have gained an invaluable insight into the practical workings of the palace kitchens, now having operated them for a total of some three months.

In his pioneering works, Dr Thurley established that the kitchens at Hampton Court provide a unique record of the archaeology and organisation of the early Tudor royal household, being the finest surviving example of a plan which had evolved from Edward IV's works at the palace of Eltham in the 1470s. The interest of the kitchens in terms of royal palace architecture is of primary importance, but they need also to be seen in a much wider context. One of the problems of putting this into effect is the very fact that they are kitchens. Most middle-class historians have until recently been dismissive of those areas occupied by servants, shut up behind the green baize door through which neither family nor houseguests would willingly enter. When talking about Tudor kitchens, academics frequently boast that they themselves cannot even boil an egg successfully, a fact that we need not question. Such ignorance of all practical creative processes may still be socially *de rigueur*, but it does not provide a sound basis from which to interpret the physical remains of the past. By contrast, anyone with a full command of their senses, especially those of touch and sight, can learn a great deal just from coming into contact with any artefact, be it an implement or a great building.

Adopting this principle, let us forget for a moment that what we are looking at here is a mere kitchen. What do we see before us? – A massive brick-built structure, rectangular in plan, and measuring over four hundred feet (122 metres) in length by ninety (27) in width. It has a broad delivery gate at one end, guarded by a security office. Pass through this, and you come to a block of offices for senior management, then long ranges of stores for raw materials, workshops large enough to employ hundreds of men, and then five large hatches, controlled by despatch offices, through which are dispensed the meals – the finished goods. What can we deduce from this? Clearly what we have here is a very substantial industrial complex, designed by people who knew all about production and management, production lines, personnel, site security and just about every other aspect of what would become established large-scale manufacturing practice. It was not until the closing decades of the eighteenth century, though, that

Britain's pioneering Industrial Revolution brought about the establishment of the world's first great factories, in which large numbers of workers were gathered together in one location in order to convert raw materials into finished goods by means of separate, sequential processes. This was quite a new concept, one that took some time to develop in the textile mills, the engineering and cutlery works, the potteries and the tanneries of the manufacturing districts.

However, whether in scale or sophistication of design, very few Georgian factories can bear favourable comparison with the Tudor kitchens at Hampton Court. Indeed, they should be seen not as mere kitchens, but as what they really are – the most important early industrial buildings in Britain, a complete Tudor factory complex, built two hundred and fifty years ahead of its time.

It is a sad fact that, at the opening of the second millennium, many people still believe that the food eaten at the Tudor court was coarse, gross, even rotten. Britain's leading cookery writers still tell us that as much of it as possible was smashed to a pulp because there were no forks, that herbs and spices were quite indiscriminately used, that their chief function was to disguise the smell and flavour of decaying meats, and that cooking fires were primitive and had a habit of going out at critical moments.[1] All these statements are totally unfounded, designed to make modern cookery appear superior – a claim which, when one looks at the facts, is difficult to justify. Remember that all Tudor food was organic, farm animals and game feeding only on natural herbage which give it a fine flavour. Similarly, all cereals, vegetables and fruits were organic, never genetically engineered, irradiated, sprayed with chemicals, coated in wax or over-processed. For this reason, organic foods should always be used, if available, when preparing Tudor recipes today. Working with these fine basic ingredients, the cooks were able to extend their centuries-old traditions, based on inventive skill and sheer professional expertise, to produce dishes of the highest quality. The fact that their recipes consist usually of little more than a list of ingredients demonstrates that they were simply aides-mémoire, for they already knew by heart all the major repertoires and finer points of technique. It is worth noting that only in recent years have some cookery books descended to the level of idiots' guides, proffering foolproof methods for boiling eggs!

Similarly, there is still a belief that the eating habits of the Tudor court were nasty and brutal. This is a pure Hollywood invention of the 1930s, originating when Charles Laughton, as Henry VIII, was seen by millions to rip legs off fowl and wolf down mouthful after mouthful, tossing the bones over his shoulder. Even today, modern costume dramas still show otherwise decorous actresses gnawing like rodents at chicken legs. And it is the same source that created 'serving wenches', regardless of the fact that, since work in the kitchens demanded the greatest muscular effort as well as a readiness to serve as trained soldiers in the King's army, women were never employed in this division of the royal household. We would be wise to view the Tudor court in the same way as Francesco Chiergató: 'In short, the wealth and civilisation of all the world are here, and those who call the English barbarians appear to render themselves such. I perceive very elegant manners and politeness.'[2]

In the following pages, the organisation and day-to-day practical activities of each kitchen department will be described in detail – they will be treated as industrial buildings staffed by industrial workers. Certainly, this is not the normal way of describing such monumental structures, but it is one that is logical and that my experience indicates as being best understood by most of the visitors who come to Hampton Court. It is very much for them that this book has been written. Having demonstrated to around 100,000 visitors to the kitchens and having answered their questions has shown me where their main areas of interest lie. I now know the kind of information that teachers want for their National Curriculum studies, which recipes are in demand for use at home, and so on. Since this is an essentially practical account, I will describe the workings of the kitchen at a single period – from 1540 to 1547, the closing years of Henry VIII's reign, when they were still in use as originally intended. I will not deal with their architectural history, because this aspect has already been fully detailed in a number of excellent publications, which are listed in the Bibliography.

For those who already know the kitchens, I hope that this book will make their workings easier to understand, while for those who want to know more about early Tudor court life and food, I hope that its descriptions and recipes will dispel many popular misconceptions and reveal a superbly organised system, carefully designed to maintain a strict social hierarchy, to develop good working practices, and to provide all the various dishes served both to Henry VIII and to his entire court.

Peter Brears
Leeds, 1999

NOTE: In the following chapters, the positions of each room, as shown in the plan and elevation of the kitchens (fig. 1), is indicated by giving its number in round brackets. Where the name of any section begins with a capital letter, as in 'the Pastry', this refers to this division of the household administration, but if it is entirely lower case, as in 'the pastry', this refers to the rooms in which its practical work was undertaken.

1

The Counting House

The Hub of the Enterprise

Today it can be difficult to comprehend the wide range of practical problems involved in operating a Tudor royal household. First, there was its great size – up to around twelve hundred people in winter and about eight hundred in summer. Then there was its importance – it was a major centre of government, the focus of international, national and personal ambitions, and our most visible national status symbol, constantly observed by ambassadors and other visitors from throughout Christendom. It was also a remarkably mobile institution, moving from palace to palace every few weeks during the winter, going on extended progresses from great house to great house in summer. To efficiently feed and manage such a complex organisation required real skill and experience, especially at a time when only carts, packhorses and barges were available for transport, roads were largely unmade, and food preservation restricted to drying and salting.

Good hospitality has always been seen as a significant indicator of a monarch's power and status. Edward IV's Black Book (1472) of royal household regulations traced its origins back to the legendary King Lud, who ensured that every day his tables were loaded with excellent, if basic foods from eight in the morning till seven in the evening, and to King Cassibellan, who supposedly organised one great feast that necessitated the slaughter of 40,000 cattle, 100,000 sheep and 30,000 deer and involved 'many disguisings, plais, minstralsye and sportes'. On somewhat safer ground, the Black Book went on to describe Henry I as a great meat-giver, Edward II as the king who could feed all his court from the beef and mutton bred in his parks, and Edward III as a great reformer of the royal household. His was 'the house of very policy, the flower of England; [he was] the first setter of certainty among his domestics upon a grounded rule'.[1] The Black Book's comprehensive regulations, or 'ordinances', were extended by Cardinal Wolsey at the palace of Eltham in 1526 and subsequently by Thomas Cromwell in 1540, each with the aim of improving the control of the household's provisions and expenditure.

Although the royal household was a complex organisation, it was basically divided into four units. The Privy Chamber served the King's personal needs, the Great Chamber those of the leading nobles and household officers, the Queen's Side served the Queen and her household, and the former Lord Steward's department provided all the provisions, equipment, fuel and major financial and catering services for most of the court. With the exception of a few separate departments, such as the Chapel Royal, the Jewel House, the Tents and Revels, the Works, the Ordnance and the Stables, which were directly responsible to the King, in 1540 the household was placed under the control of a Lord Great Master. Here we shall see how he and his staff administered the former Lord Steward's department at just one of Henry VIII's palaces, Hampton Court.

When you approach the long Tudor west front of Hampton Court Palace, you see the façade of Wolsey's Base Court lodgings flanked by two projecting wings. The one on the right was the Great House of Ease, or latrine block, while the one on the left was the Back Gate, the entrance to the main kitchen buildings. Here, on the first floor above the gate passage, was the Counting House, the administrative centre of the royal household. In the Black Book its purpose had been defined as the maintenance of

> worship and welfare of the hoole household . . . in whyche the corrections and judgements by gevyn; in whome ys taken the audyte of all thinges of thys courte, beying of the [Treasurer's] charge, as principal hedde of all other officers in whom every officer of the household takyth hys charge on hys knee, promissing trouthe and obedyance to the King, and to the rules of thys office; for at the green-cloth ys alwey represented the Kinges power touching matters of thys household.[2]

To stress this power, the Counting House bore its own coat of arms – a key and a white rod arranged as a diagonal cross, indicating its right to open, close, and administer justice to all household offices. These devices were set on a green background to represent the 'greencloth', the table covered in green baize which stood in the centre of the counting house, around which all the chief officers sat when transacting their business. This is how its component parts are described in the building accounts:[3]

> A pair of timbers for a table in the newe counting house . . .
> for an iron trestle for the same table . . .

for 2 locks for the cupboard in the same table . . .
for 6 heart rings [handles] for the tills [drawers] in the same table.

As head of the entire household, the Lord Great Master presided at the greencloth. This important post was first held by Charles Brandon, Duke of Suffolk, from 1540 to 1545, and then by William Paulet, Lord St John. These nobles were directly responsible to the King for regulating every aspect of his household, enforcing and introducing appropriate financial and management regulations, defining the duties of all their officers, reducing waste, ensuring efficiency, and disciplining those who infringed the numerous rules.

Second in command came the Treasurer of the Household, Sir Thomas Cheney. He was similarly responsible for the regulation and supply of the household, the Black Book describing how on taking up his appointment he should make a full inventory of all the goods placed in his care, oversee the acquisition of food, forage, fuel, wines and so on, make sure that everything in his office was efficiently controlled and run, as well as administering justice over his household staff – 'cheryssing the good officer, and punishing the evyll doer' as necessary.[4]

In third place, Sir John Gage served the Treasurer as Comptroller of the Household. It was his job to keep detailed accounts 'as of every pewter dysshe, cup of tree [wood], pottes of leather or earth, as of othyr many small and infinite spyces and other thinges', such as foodstuffs, gold and silver. He also managed the Treasurer's finances, agreed the specifications and prices of goods supplied to the household, ordered the payment of accounts from the various domestic offices, audited their returns, reported on their performance, and listed the items remaining in them when the court moved on to another property.[5]

Each of these great officers held his position by the direct authority of the King as represented by a white staff of office – hence their combined title of the White Sticks. In practice, they supervised the overall management of the household, at least one of the three having to be present at the greencloth in the counting house between eight and nine each morning to inspect its financial records, uncover any unreasonable wastage, and punish those responsible for incurring it.[6] The White Sticks also determined the remuneration of all the household staff. Senior staff, such as the cofferer, were paid an annual sum, in his case £50 a year, while the junior staff, such as sergeants and clerks, or yeomen, grooms and pages, received a daily rate of 16d and 6d respectively when on duty, and 'board wages' (a subsistence allowance) of 6d and 4d respectively, if they were sick.[7] Of greater importance, however, was the granting of 'bouche of court' – the right to receive food and other necessaries from the court. Those entitled to this privilege were listed in an 'ordinary' prepared by the officers of the Greencloth – this was a document stating precisely what each person should receive according to his rank.[8] A duke, for example, received:

> every of them for their Bouche of Court in the morning one chett lofe [brown loaf], one manchett [small white loaf], one gallon of ale; for the afternoone, one manchett, one gallon of ale; and after supper, one chet lofe, one manchet, one gallon of ale, one pitcher of wyne, and from the last day of October unto the first day of April, one torch, one pricket [candle], two sises [small candles], one pound of white lights, ten talshides [timbers for fuel], eight faggots and . . . from the last day of March unto the first day of November, to have moyety [half] of the said waxe, white lights, wood and coals, which doth amount in money by the year to the summe of £39 13s 4d.

At the other end of the scale, ordinary officers of the household received:[9]

> For their Bouche after supper, everie of them being lodged within the court, dim' [half] chet lofe, dim' gallon of ale; and from the last day of October unto the first day of Aprill, by the day, two sises, one pound white lights, two talhides, two faggots; and from the last day of March unto the first day of November, to have the moyety of the said waxe, white lights, wood and coals, amounting to the sum of £4 7s 5d.

The ordinary also listed those entitled to have both bouche of court and their dinners and suppers (to be either consumed in the King's Chamber or in the Queen's Side, or with the remainder of the household), and those who were entitled only to their food and wages. The details of each individual's menu were minutely specified, with regard both to content and to cost, the King's and Queen's costing a massive £3 5s 0d daily, while that of a servant or porter cost about 2¼d.[10] Just how much it could cost to feed the entire court for a year is given in an ordinary of the 1540s, which details an expenditure of £16,327 5s 5d on food alone, and a further £4,445 2s 6d on the transport costs, fuel and equipment required for its acquisition and preparation.[11]

To control these sums efficiently the White Sticks were assisted by the cofferer, the most senior professional officer, who was the effective working head of the administration. If the Lord Great Master could be called the chairman of the board, the cofferer was the chief executive, directly responsible for obtaining the necessary funding through such bodies as the Courts of Augmentation, First Fruits and Tenths, Woods and Liveries, and also for annually submitting the book of accounts, along with the 'book of comptrolment', to the Exchequer, the office to which he was ultimately accountable for the administration of the household.[12] The White Sticks were also advised by three clerks of the greencloth, three clerks comptroller and four masters of the household – two for the King's Chamber and two for the Queen's Side. In order to ensure that the household staff were 'less pestered' and to ease the problems of lodging large numbers of officers at court, only two of the masters of the household, one clerk of the kitchen and one clerk of the spicery were on duty at any one time; these worked in six-week rotating shifts, and were paid board wages for the time spent away from the court.[13]

In order to provision the household, the clerk of the kitchen drew up lists of what would be required over the coming week in the kitchen offices, which included the Kitchens themselves, the Buttery, the Cellar, the Pantry, the Poultry, the Pastry and the Saucery, the Scullery and the Woodyard. Similarly the clerk of the spicery prepared lists of provisions for the Spicery, the Chandlery, the Confectionary, the Ewery, the Wafery and the Laundry once every month. These lists were submitted to the Greencloth for inspection, and then passed to the cofferer, who issued them to the 'purveyors', the purchasing officers of each individual office. The cofferer also provided the purveyors with an 'imprest', or advance of money, so that they could acquire the items specified. The provision of all the beef, mutton, veal and pork, and the fresh, sea- and salt-fish which made up the bulk of the household's diet, was the task of a separate office, the Acatery. As with other commodities, the prices to be paid were first agreed with the officers of the greencloth, usually at below market prices.[14] Bearing the King's commission to compulsorily purchase the required supplies, the sergeant of the acatery, accompanied by a clerk comptroller, attended fairs and markets with the ready money provided by the cofferer, so as to buy his livestock at the most advantageous price. Also, they both travelled to the coast every year to arrange the purchase of all their ling (a kind of cod), ordinary cod, and other fish. Here it became more convenient and economical to enter into a contract with an individual supplier, as when Thomas Hewyt of Hythe in Kent agreed to provide the household with a whole range of fish at previously agreed prices.[15]

As the various goods arrived at the palace, they would be checked for value, quality and quantity by the clerks comptroller. To ensure that they could perform this task accurately, the Black Book had given them the responsibility of checking the measures of all the vessels used, from the hefty tuns, vats, butts, pipes, hogsheads, rundlets (casks) and barrels down to the smallest measures such as pots of wine and all sorts of other vessels such as bottles, bushels, half-bushels and pecks.[16] Similarly, all the wheat arriving at the bakehouse, the wax, the linen, the fruit and so on arriving at the spicery, the wine, beer and ale delivered to the cellars, and every other commodity too, was either accepted as satisfactory for use or rejected – in which case the purveyor would be penalised appropriately. The clerks comptroller then entered details of every incoming item in their book of records. This they would bring to the greencloth, so that the accounts could be passed for payment and the fresh deliveries compared with the 'briefs' which recorded the daily consumption. As a further control, each purveyor provided the clerk of his particular office with a complete list, or 'parcel' of the purchases he had made during the previous month, which was then passed to the clerk comptroller, via the clerk of the greencloth, for checking and entering in a book of foot of parcels. Here the word 'foot' referred to what was written at the foot of the accounts, the sum or total from each parcel, from which the annual expenditure was calculated. In addition, the clerk of the kitchen submitted his yearly accounts to the greencloth within two months of the year's end, including details of outstanding creditors and any petitions for the reimbursement of any additional items of expenditure incurred during the year.

By all these means a reasonably close control of the household's expenditure could be maintained. But this represented only one part of the Greencloth's responsibilities. It was also in charge of the distribution and use of all provisions, which entailed keeping wastage and pilfering to a minimum – essential at a time when cooks were notorious for their prodigal personal consumption and willingness to feed their cronies at their master's expense. According to one observer writing in 1509:[17]

These fools revelling in their master's cost
Spare no expence, not caring his damage,
But they as caitifs often thus them boast
In their gluttony, with dissolute language:
'Be merry, companions, and lusty of courage,
We have our pleasure in dainty meat and drink,
On which things we always muse and think.'

'Eat we and drink we therefore without all care,
With revel without measure, as long as we may.
It is a royal thing thus lustily to fare
With others meat, thus revel we alway,
Spare not the pot, another shall it pay.
When that is done, spare not for more to call.
He merely sleeps, the which shall pay for all.'

The great deceit, guile and uncleanliness
Of any scullion, or any bawdy cook,

His lord abusing for his unthriftiness.
Some for the nonce their meat lewdly dress,
Giving it a taste too sweet, too salt, or strong,
Because the servants would eat it them among . . .

And with what meats soever the lord shall fare,
If it be in the kitchen before it comes to the hall,
The cook and scullion must taste it first of all.
In every dish the caitifs have their hands,
Gaping as it were dogs for a bone.
When nature is content, few of them understands,
In so much that, as I trow, of them is none
That dye for age, but by gluttony each one.

The main way of preventing such abuses was to prepare detailed briefs of what had been used by the household every single day. By eight in the morning the clerk of the kitchen had to be at the greencloth with the briefs for the Kitchen, the Buttery, the Cellar, the Poultry, the Scullery and the Woodyard, the Pastry and the Saucery, and the clerk of the spicery had to be there with those of the Spicery, Chandlery, Confectionary, Ewery, Wafery and Laundry. Similarly, the acatery clerk brought in his itemised accounts for the meats and so on that had been used on the previous day. Before 9 a.m. these briefs had been inspected by the clerk of the greencloth and clerk comptroller, after which the former, in the presence of the cofferer, had to engross them – that is, transcribe a summary of each one into a parchment main docket (the main record of the household's daily consumption) – before dinner was served at ten.[18]

Virtually all this accounting procedure took place either in the Counting House over the Back Gate, or in the offices of the comptroller, the cofferer, the clerk of the greencloth, clerk comptroller, clerk of the kitchen and clerk of the spicery, which were all arranged on the first floor of the Greencloth Yard. The security of these offices, and of their contents, was placed in the charge of the yeoman and groom of the counting house: these two would be illiterate, preferably, to ensure that they could not convey confidential information to people outside their office.[19] They had to prepare the counting house for the day's business by eight every morning, and ensure the safekeeping of all its books and records. No officer was allowed to remove any of the accounts without the consent of at least two or three officers of the greencloth, who were then directly responsible for overseeing their prompt return. It would be a mistake, however, to believe that the officers of the greencloth were solely office-bound administrators, for their duties took them daily into the various working offices.

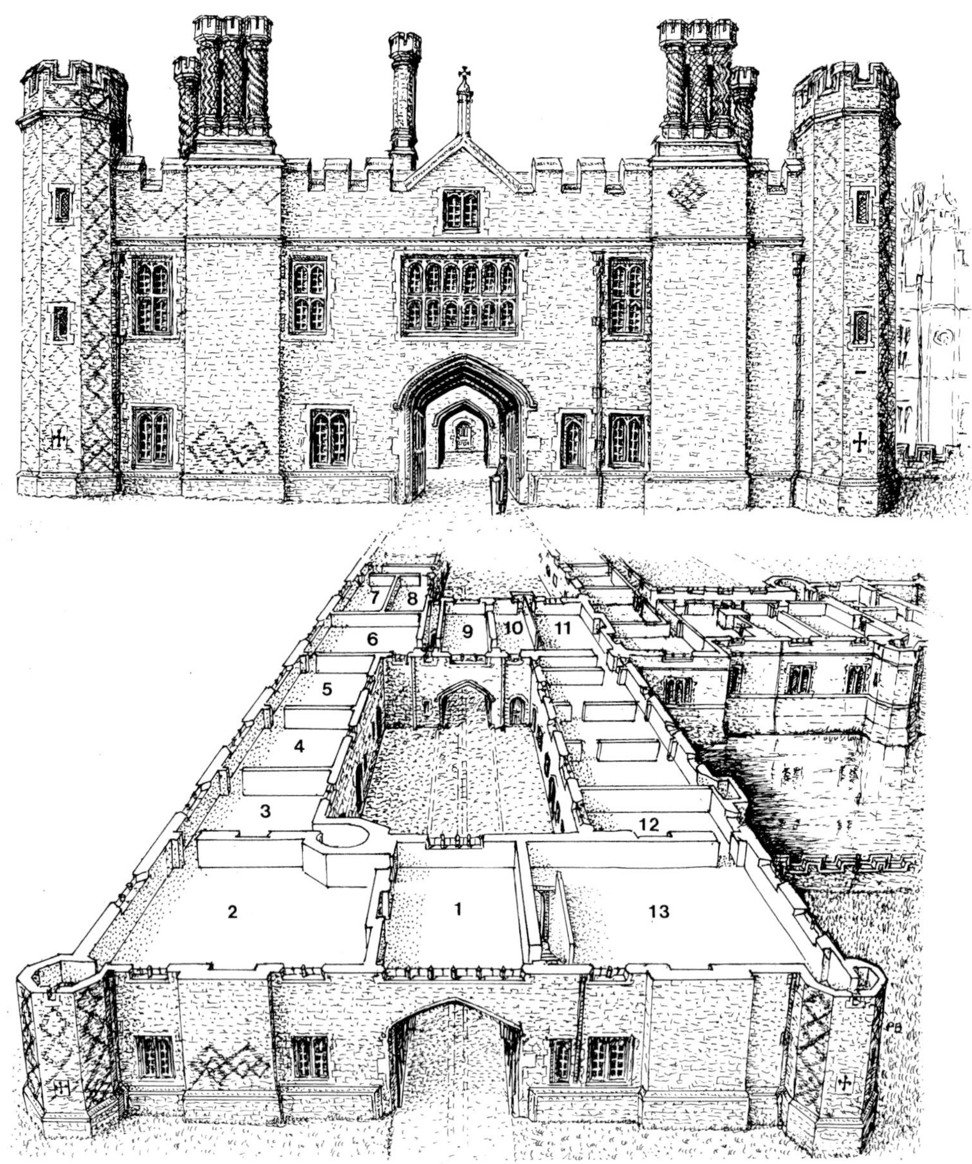

2. *The Back Gate and the Counting House* The royal household was administered from the offices of the Counting House, which occupied the first floor above the Back Gate and around the Greencloth Yard. These rooms were occupied by:

1. Counting House (the Greencloth)
2–5. Comptroller's lodgings
6. Scullery office
7,8. Pastry office
9. Clerk of the kitchen's office
10,11. Clerks comptroller
12,13. Cofferer

One of the most remarkable aspects of the kitchens at Hampton Court is the way they were designed to accommodate the needs of the administrators. If we assume that the various rooms identified in a survey of the lodgings of Hampton Court, taken on 4 August, 1674, had retained their original mid sixteenth century purpose – which seems reasonable in view of the conservative nature of the organisation and the lack of any substantial body of conflicting evidence – a very efficient plan soon becomes evident.[20]

The placing of the offices on the first floor of the Greencloth Yard, for example, ensured that all the officers could clearly see everyone and everything entering or leaving the premises. More particularly, the clerk of the scullery and woodyard could watch the door of the coal cellar, which lay just beneath his window. And by looking westwards from their offices, both the clerk comptroller and the clerk of the kitchen could keep an eye on the doors of the fish larder, the confectionary, the pastry and the boiling house, the latter giving sole access into the main larders and kitchens.

Every day the clerk of the greencloth, the clerk comptroller and the clerk of the kitchen, attended by the officers of the larder, would go into the larders, to check what remained of the previous day's supplies and what had been recently delivered by the Acatery and the Poultry.[21] There they selected which meat and fish were to be prepared that day and issued them to the King's, the Queen's and the household's master cooks, along with instructions regarding the way they were to be dressed, so that the meat was 'neither over much boyled or rosted'.[22] All this business had to be transacted at appropriate times so that the cooks had enough time to prepare the food for the main 10 a.m. and 4 p.m. meals.[23] For this reason, the Black Book had instructed the clerks 'to be at couplage [cutting] of fleyshe . . . in the grete larder, as requiryth nightly to know the portion of beef and moton for the expences of the next day'.[24] They had also to be there well before eight every morning to check in the poultry and so forth.

Just before the meals were served, the clerk of the greencloth, the clerk comptroller and the clerk of the kitchen, probably with further clerical assistance, took up their positions in the specially designed offices next to the 'dressers', the serving hatches where the food was passed out from the kitchens into the hands of the waiters.[25] The dressers which served the Great Hall, where most of the household ate, were located at the south-west corner of the kitchens (no. 34). Here the dresser office, a large room heated by its own fireplace, had a broad hatch which faced across the serving area, so that the clerks, joined here by the clerk of the larder, could see that the correct quantities of the relatively basic foods that were served here were dispensed at every course.[26] At the east end of the kitchens, meanwhile, a much more sophisticated dresser office (no. 42) was recording the finer foods served for the Council Chamber and the Great Chamber (or 'Great Watching Chamber'). From the north wall of this office, a vertical opening enabled the clerks to see across the inner side of the serving hatches, while also keeping watch on the kitchen door into the serving area and the wide service door leading towards the orchards to the north, thereby ensuring total security at the outer end of the kitchen offices. And when the hatches were opened, a further hatch in the east wall of the dresser office gave the clerks a direct view that enabled them to count all the outgoing dishes, not only from the main kitchens but also from the separate kitchen on the opposite side of the large servery area called the Great Space.

The Counting House also managed all the household's personnel matters. The payment of wages, fees and board wages, for example, was the responsibility of the cofferer. To enable him to carry out this task, the clerks comptroller drew up a parchment check-roll every quarter, recording the names of every member of staff employed within the household. This was used to check everyone's daily presence in their place of work, to confirm that those who should eat in the King's or Queen's chambers actually did so rather than eating privately elsewhere, and that those who had obtained leave of absence from one of the White Sticks returned to their duties by the agreed date.[27] In this way it was possible to dock the wages of all those who did not report for work. For accounting purposes, the clerks comptroller entered the payment of wages and board wages in their standing ledger, along with the purchase of provisions. They also checked whether more servants were being employed than were listed in the approved ordinances, the 'establishment lists', and whether any unauthorised strangers or vagabonds were being retained within the household. If such were found, the sergeant or head of the offending office was admonished and warned that if he did not immediately rectify the situation he would lose two days' wages. For other infringements of their rules, the senior officers of the greencloth could enforce discipline, first by giving the offender a fair warning at the greencloth table; if this proved ineffective, it would be followed by the loss of a month's wages, then imprisonment for a month; and as a last resort, exclusion from the court for ever. Also, anyone who was habitually drunk had his keys removed, and was denied access to any of the household's provisions until he had reformed.[28]

As all this clearly shows, much thought and organisational experience went into the management of the royal household, every opportunity being taken to ensure that it functioned as efficiently as possible.

2

Serving the Court

Numbers, Quantities, Costs

Before moving on into the kitchens themselves, it is worth taking a close look at the food they had to produce. For a start, the bulk of it consisted of meat, poultry and game from Sundays to Thursdays, and fish on Fridays and Saturdays as well as during Lent and for other specified feasts. Bread was eaten with every meal, and ale and wine were the main drinks.

Unlike today, when we tend to think of communal meals in terms of so many individual settings, portions, or 'covers', Tudor cooks worked in terms of 'messes', meaning a whole menu for a small group of people, all eating together (and not a reflection of the messy state of the food!). Usually a mess was intended for four, but its size and quality could vary enormously. The King's dinner was exceptional in that it comprised a single mess of thirteen dishes costing a total of 8s 8d, while that of the servants, for example, had just two dishes and cost 8d.[1] More specifically, the word 'mess' was also used to describe each single dish, so that the 'mess' in the sense of 'menu' was made up of a number of individual messes of beef, mutton, veal, tarts, fruit and so on, each being sufficient for the whole 'mess' of four or more people dining together.

This was a very practical arrangement, for a variety of reasons. To begin with, once the number of people expected for a meal had been determined, it was a simple matter to divide it by four to work out the number of messes. The clerks could then issue this number of joints to the cooks, and later count them out at the dresser after they had been cooked. Similarly, the number needed of every other dish could be quickly calculated, so that the required number of serving dishes could be made ready. Meanwhile, those setting up the tables and arranging the tableware knew precisely how many tables, cloths, napkins, spoons, bowls and so on had to be set out.

In some cases, the content of a specific mess is given in the household ordinances. Those served to the senior members of the household staff reflect their differing statuses and the number of people they were expected to entertain at their table:[2]

Dish	*Lord Great Master*	*Treasurer and Comptroller*
Heron	1 mess, 4 birds	1 mess, 1 bird
Bittern	1 mess, 4 birds	
Curlew	1 mess, 4 birds	
Chickens	1 mess, 12 birds	
Cocks	1 mess, 12 birds	1 mess, 3 birds
Plovers	1 mess, 12 birds	1 mess, 4 birds
Snipes	1 mess, 9 birds	
Larks	1 mess, 48 birds	
Rabbits	1 mess, 12 carcases	
Lamb	1 mess, 1 carcase	1 mess, half carcase

Another way of calculating the size of the messes is to compare their costs as recorded in the household ordinances with the cost of their raw materials. In 1549, for example, the Court of Aldermen of the City of London enforced the following price lists both in their 'shambles' or butcher's shops, and in their markets:[3]

best beef, maximum price,	3½d per pound
best mutton, maximum price	1½d per pound
other mutton, maximum price	1¼d per pound
best veal, maximum price	6s 8d the carcase

Using these figures as a guide, messes of beef for the majority of the household, recorded as costing 6d or 8d in the ordinances, would weigh around 2lb (900g) raw and therefore some 1lb 8oz (700g) cooked, giving each person around 6oz (175g) of cooked beef to every meal. Priced at 3d, the messes of mutton would also weigh around 2lb, while the veal priced at 4d (assuming a 60lb (27kg) dressed carcase) would weigh around 3lb (1350g).[4] Although approximate, these estimates show that most officers, yeomen and grooms – the bulk of the household staff – would be eating over 2lb 7oz (1100g) of meat every day:

Dinner per mess	*Probable raw weight*
Beef	2lb
Veal	3lb
Other meats	(2lb?)

Supper per mess	*Probable raw weight*
Beef	2lb
Mutton	2lb
Other meats	(2lb?)
Total meat per mess daily	13lb
Less 25% shrinkage	–3lb 4oz
Total weight, cooked	9lb 12oz
If 4 people per mess	2lb 7oz daily consumption of meat

Similar quantities were prepared for the senior officers, the courtiers and the King, but, as already mentioned, for them the range of dishes and quality were far superior, as were their methods of preparation.

Food and drink have always been very important status symbols: not only can they demonstrate the power, wealth and taste of the host, but they also give him a unique opportunity to define the social standing of everyone eating at his tables. In the Tudor court, the place where people took their meals, the number and content of their dishes, and the design and materials of their tableware, were all aimed at maintaining a rigid hierarchy. So, at Hampton Court as at other royal palaces, there was no attempt to disguise the differences between the various levels of importance; on the contrary, they were made as obvious as possible to everyone dining there.

One of the best descriptions of this practice is given by Alexander Barkeley (1475–1552), poet and scholar, who appears to have come to court and dined in the Great Hall as a very observant stranger. He was the same 'Maister Barkleye, the black monke and poete' whom Wolsey was asked to despatch to the Field of the Cloth of Gold in 1520, to devise verses to decorate the great temporary banqueting house for the entertainment of Henry VIII, Catherine of Aragon and Francis I, King of France. Writing in the early years of Henry's reign, Barkeley first noted that:[5]

> . . . though white and brown [bread] be both at one price
> With brown shalt thou feed, lest white make thee nice [refined].
> The Lords will alway that people note and see
> Between them and servants some diversity;
> Though it to them turn to no profit at all,
> If they have pleasure, the servant shall have small.

The inferiority of the food served to him personally became particularly obvious when the waiters walked through the Hall, bearing the finest dishes, and took them up to the great ones seated on the raised dais at its upper end, and probably to those in the Great Watching Chamber beyond, too:

> For this unto courtiers most commonly doth hap,
> That while they have brown bread and cheese in their lap,
> On it fast gnawing as hounds ravenous,
> Anon by them passes of meat delicious,
> And costly dishes a score may they tell;
> Their greedy gorges are wrapt with the smell;
> The daintious dishes which pass through the hall
> It were a great labour for me to name them all . . .
> [And] when these courtiers sit on benches idle,
> Smelling those dishes, they bite upon the bridle,
> And then is their pain and anger fell as gall,
> When all passeth by, and they have none at all.
> What fish is of savour sweet and delicious
> When thou sore hungerest, thy prince hath plenteous;
> Roasted or sodden [boiled] in sweet herbs or wine,
> Or fried in oil most saperous and fine.
> Such fish to behold, and none thereof to taste,
> Pure envy causeth, thy heart near to burst;
> Then seeing his dishes of flesh new again,
> Thy mind hath torment, yet with much great pain,
> Well mayest thou smell the pasties of a hart
> And diverse dainties, but nought shall be thy part.
> The crane, the pheasant, the peacock and curlew,
> The partridge, plover, bittern and heronshew [small heron].
> Each bird of the air and beast of the ground
> At prince's pleasure shalt thou behold abound,
> Seasoned so well in liquor redolent
> That the hall is full of pleasant smell and scent;
> To see such dishes and smell the sweet odour,
> And nothing to taste, is utter displeasure.

Sometimes the senior courtiers, to demonstrate their patronage but also to make sure their inferiors fully appreciated what they were missing, sent tasty delicacies down to those dining in the body of the Hall:

> To thy next fellow some morsel may be sent
> To thy displeasure, great anguish and torment
> Whereby in thy mind thou mayest suspect and trow [believe]

Him more in favour, and in contempt then thou,
And sometimes to thee is sent a little [s]crap
With savour thereof to take thee in the trap,
Not to allay thy hunger and desire,
But by the sweetness to set thee more on fire.

The contemporary dietaries show that Barkeley's observations had more to do with fact than with mere poetic conceit.

At the bottom of the scale came the servants, porters, scourers and turnbroaches (spit-turners), and the children of the various domestic officers. They took their meals of bread, beef, mutton, veal (or ling and other seafish for fish days) and ale on the shop floor, so to speak, where they worked.[6] Next came the officers, sergeants, clerks, yeomen, porters and grooms, most of whom dined in the Great Hall, the 'works canteen', on a similar menu, but with the addition of the more delicate lamb, goose and coney, or cod, plaice and whiting on fish days. The senior members of the household dined at the upper end of the hall, in the King's Great Chamber or Watching Chamber, and in the King's Council Chamber, the 'executive staff restaurant' of the palace.[7] For them there was far better food, including:[8]

Meat and poultry	*Fish*	*Sweet dishes*
beef	purpoise	tarts
mutton	bream	doucets (sweet flans)
veal	lamprey	fritters
lamb	plaice	fryaundes ('delicacies')
kid	gurnard	fruit
rabbits (young)	byrt (turbot)	butter
conies (full-grown rabbits)	tench	eggs
heron	whiting	
bittern	haddock	
curlew	sole	
teal	pike	
pigeon	salmon	
sea-mew (common gull)	ling	
gull (other species)	chevin (chub)	
plover		
lark		
snipe		
cock		
chicken		
capon		

All of this was cooked in the main household kitchens, but in addition there were the Privy Kitchens, which prepared all the food for the King's and his Queen's personal tables. Henry VIII's lay just below his Long Gallery, close to his Privy Chamber, or 'director's dining-room'. The royal diet included everything in the list above, but with the addition of these luxuries:[9]

Meat	*Fish*	*Sweet dishes*
venison pasty	sturgeon	custard
venison haunch	seal	garnished custard
venison in bruet (broth)	calver salmon	jelly
venison rascals	eel with lamprey	cream of almonds
red deer haunch	carp	closed tarts
godwit	trout	baked pippins
pheasant	perch	baked oranges
shoveller	crayfish	fruit with powder (ground spices)
partridge	mullet	fruit with 'piscards' (?)
quail	bass	oranges
sparrow	salt-eel	quinces
stork	salt-lamprey	pippins
swan	crabs	
goose	lobsters	
pullet	shrimps	
	herrings	

Having to prepare most of these dishes virtually every day of the year presented major problems for the kitchen staff. As a Spanish visitor to the court noted only a few years later, in 1554:[10]

> The Queen spends over 300,000 ducats a year on her table, for all the thirteen councillors eat in the palace, as well as the household officers, the master of the horse, the master of the household, the Queen's as well as our own . . . and the wives of these gentlemen into the bargain. The Queen's ladies also eat by themselves in the palace, and their servants, as well as the councillors', governors' and household officers', and then there are the 200 men of the guard . . . There are usually eighteen kitchens in full blast, and they seem veritable hells, such is the stir and bustle in them . . . the usual daily consumption is eighty to one hundred sheep – and the sheep here are very big and fat – a dozen fat beeves, a dozen and a half of calves, without mentioning poultry, game, deer, boars and great numbers of rabbits. There is

> plenty of beer here, and they drink more than would fill the Valladolid river . . .

Even for such a great household, 'eighteen kitchens in full blast' sounds like an exaggeration, but there is no doubt that eighteen was the number of major rooms in permanent use whenever the court was resident at Hampton Court. Moving inwards from the park, they are:

Outer Court:	poultry, bakehouse, privy bakehouse	3
Pastry Yard:	confectionary, 3 pastry rooms	4
Fish Court:	boiling house, 3 larders	4
Kitchen:	2 hall-place kitchen-workhouses, hall-place kitchen, Lord's side kitchen, Lord's side workhouse, 2 privy kitchens	7
	Total	18

The hall-place kitchens prepared all the basic foods for the lower ranks of the household, who ate in the Great Hall, while the Lord's side kitchen provided better fare for those dining at the Lord Great Master's table, and sometimes that of the Lord Chamberlain. The best food of all was cooked in the King's and Queens' privy kitchens.

We shall now visit each of these offices in turn, to find out more about their equipment and their operation.

3

The Outer Court

Poultry, Bakehouse, Woodyard

From the medieval period through to the late nineteenth century, bakehouses and similar places that produced smoke, smells, potential fire risks and a bustle of activity at unsocial hours were located in the outbuildings of most great houses. This was certainly the case at Hampton Court, where a block of outer offices was built in the Outer Court, the present lawned area extending from the entrance gates along to the main west front of the palace (fig. 3).

Construction started in the spring of 1529 at the east end, incorporating materials from Wolsey's old bakehouse in the park, while new timber frames were prefabricated at Reigate by a carpenter called John Wylton.[1] These were carted to Hampton Court, then erected to form 'a ryshe house [for rushes] . . . a grete bakehouwse and a prevey bakehouse with a crosse howse betwn them . . . a brede howse, a panlever [?] and a scalding house'. The yard walls, chimney-stacks and ovens were built in brick for additional security and fire protection, while the roofs were covered in earthenware tiles by one William Garret in November 1529. All this is clear evidence that the whole of this large building, measuring some 300 feet (91m) by 90 feet (27m), was constructed within some seven months.

✿

The west, or outer, end of these offices was occupied by the Poultry and Scalding House, which was controlled by the sergeant of the poultry and his clerk. All the birds required for both the King and his household were purchased around London and beyond by two yeomen purveyors, using a scale of set prices which was revised from time to time as the economy dictated. Those confirmed by the Lord Great Master and the Counting House for William Gurley, purveyor of poultry, on 27 March 1545, were as follows:[2]

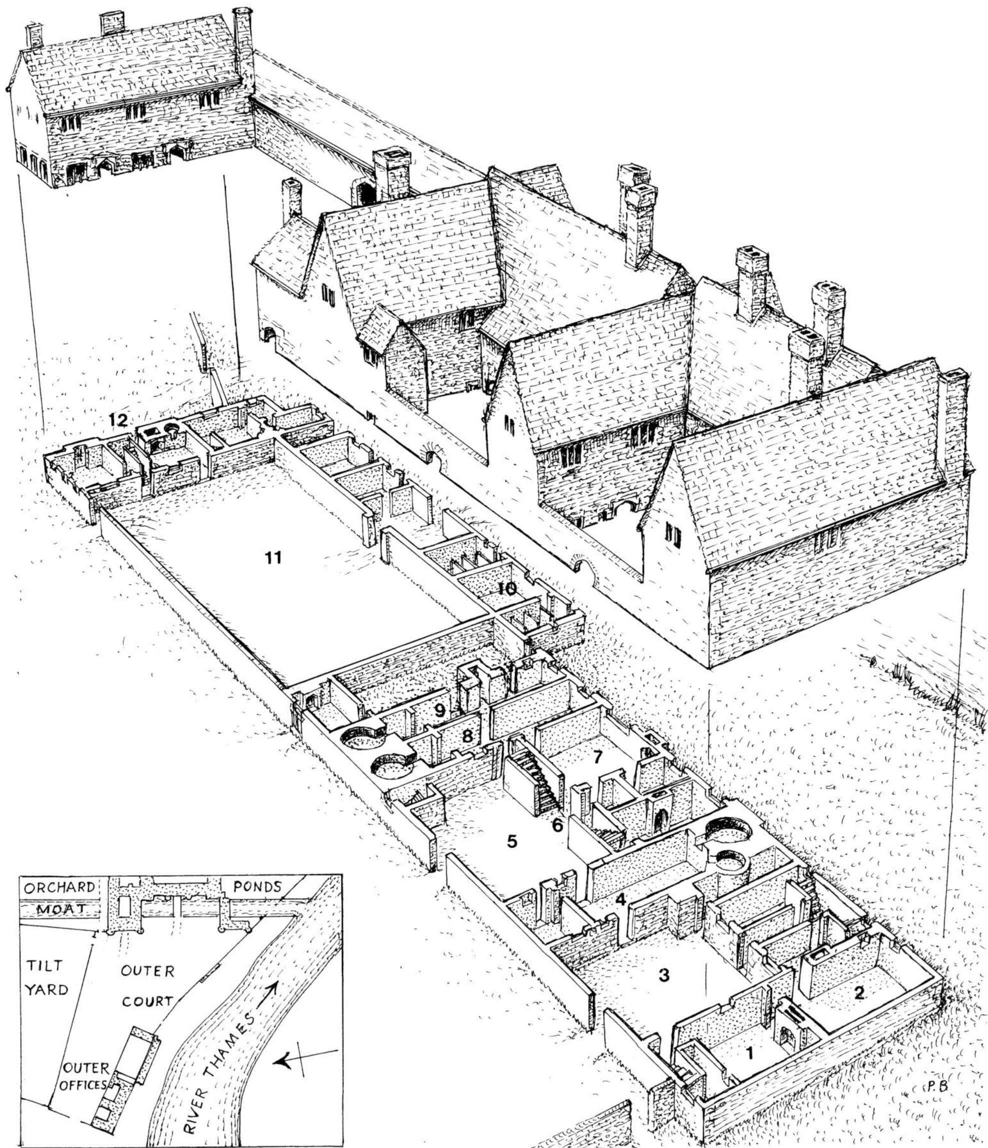

3. *The houses of office* Situated in the Outer Court (the present lawned area in front of the Great Gatehouse), this timber structure of 1529–30 was built with brick ovens and chimney-stacks to accommodate the Scalding House for preparing poultry and rabbits, the Bakehouse for breadmaking, and the Woodyard for preparing and storing wood, fuel and rushes.

1, 2. Scalding Rooms (?)
3. Poultry Yard
4. Privy Bakehouse
5. Bakehouse Yard
6. Stairs up to granaries
7. Bread House (?)
8, 9. Great Bakehouse
10. Stables for purveyors' horses
11. The Woodyard
12. The Woodyard Offices

Swannes, the peice	6s
Cranes, Storke, Bustard, the peice	4s 8d
Capons of gress [fat], the peice	22d
Capons good, the peice	14d
Capons, Kent, the peice	8d
Hennes of gress . . . the peice	7d
House Rabbetts, the peice	3d
Rabats out of the Warren . . .	2½d
Ronners [free-range rabbits], the peice	2d
Wynter Conies, the peice	2½d
Herons, Shovelard [shovellers], Byttorne	20d
Mallards, the peice	4d
Kyddes, the peice	2s
Pegions, the dozen	10d
Large and fat geese from Easter till Midsummer, the peice	7d
Geese of gress from Lamas till 22th day, the peice	8d
Eggs from Shrovetide, till Michaelmas, the hundred	14d
Eggs from Michaelmas till Shrovetide, the hundred	20d
Peacocks and Peachicks	16d
Grewes [grebes], Egretts, the peice	14d
Gulles, the peice	16d
Mewes, the peice	8d
Godwits, the peice	14d
Dottrells, the peice	4d
Quails, very fat, the peice	4d
Cocks, the peice	4d
Plovers, the peice	3d
Snytes [snipes], the peice	2½d
Larks, the dozen	6d
Teales, the peice	2d
Wigeons, the peice	3d
Sparrows, the dozen	4d
Butter, sweet, the pound	3d

Although some of these items are still cooked and eaten today, many have not appeared on English menus for centuries. Relatively few descriptions of their basic preparation survive, and I include some of them here. As a Venetian visitor to England around 1500 recalled, 'It is a truly beautiful thing to behold one or two thousand swans upon the river Tames . . . which are eaten by the English like ducks and geese.'[3] Although eaten in most great households, particularly around Christmas and the New Year, large swans were usually fairly tough and could have a fishy taste. The cygnets made much better eating, and are still served with great ceremony by Mr Swan Warden at the annual feast of the Vintners' Company of London.[4] Among the large wading birds, the heron, bittern and shoveller were all highly regarded, the bittern in particular having much the flavour of the hare, and none of the fishiness of the heron. In his *Castel of Helth* of 1541, Sir Thomas Elyot, diplomat and writer, stated that these birds 'being yonge and fatte, be lyghtyer digested than the Crane, and the Byttour sooner than the Hearon . . . All these fowles muste be eaten with muche ginger or pepper, and have good old wyne drunk after them.'[5] The stork was certainly a much rarer bird, but, according to the medical writer Tobias Venner's *Via Recta ad Vitam Longam* of 1620, it 'is of hard substance, of a wilde savour, and of very naughty juyce'![6] Both the snipe and the godwit, smaller waders, made very good eating. According to Sir Thomas Browne, physician and writer, Godwits . . . [are] accounted the daintiest dish in England; and, I think, for bigness, of the biggest price.'[7] As for ducks, the wigeon and the smaller teal were greatly appreciated too – 'Teal for pleasantnesse and wholesomeness excelleth all other water fowle',[8] commented Venner.

The appearance on the list of seabirds such as mews (common gulls), gulls and puffins may surprise us, but in fact they had all been eaten for centuries. The puffin's flesh tasted so fishy that one writer in 1530 described it as 'a fysshe lyke a teele', and the Church actually classed them as fishes which could be eaten in Lent.[9] In Cornwall puffins were chased out of their holes near the cliffs using ferrets and then, being 'exceeding fat, [they were] kept salted, and reputed for fish, as coming neerest thereto in taste'.[10] Prepared in this way, they were considered something of a delicacy. Gulls, meanwhile, were caught in nets and fattened during the winter in poultry yards, where they were 'crammed with salt beef ready for the table'.[11]

Of the wild land birds, the most impressive was the great bustard, the largest wild bird in Europe. Before it became extinct in this country around 1860, it was remembered as having particularly delicious flesh, weighing some fifteen pounds or more, with a six-foot wing span.[12] The much smaller quail, plover and dotterel were equally desirable, especially the first of the three – fat and tender, it was lured into nets using a whistle called a quail-pipe.[13] In contrast, the delicate yet nourishing larks were taken either by a small hawk called a hobby, or by using a mirror and a piece of red cloth to distract them until they were netted. In Shakespeare's *King Henry the Eighth* the Earl of Surrey alludes to this practice when taunting Cardinal Wolsey about his red cardinal's hat:[14]

> If we live thus tamely,
> To be thus jaded by a piece of scarlet,
> Farewell nobility! Let his grace go forward
> And dare us with his cap like larks.

The lark was considered to be 'of all smale byrdes the beste', whereas sparrows were 'harde to digest, and are very hot, and stirreth up Venus, and specially the brains of them', Sir Thomas Elyot tells us.[15] Presumably this is why they were a luxury at the palace, while remaining a poor man's food, netted and caught beneath sieves from the earliest times through to the middle of the twentieth century.[16]

Of the tame birds, many of the geese, hens and pheasants, for instance, were fed in the poultry yards attached to some of the palaces, as well as being purchased in vast numbers. Peacocks and peachicks made very impressive dishes at table, but had to be eaten when still quite young. Dr Andrew Boorde, physician and traveller, states in his *Dyetary of Helth* (1542) that 'yonge peechyken of half a yere of age be praysed, olde pecockes be harde of dygestyon', while Henry Buttes complained of their 'very harde meate, of bad temperature, & as evil juyce. Wonderously increaseth melancholy, & casteth, as it were, a clowd upon the minde'.[17] However, when a year-old bird was recently roasted at Hampton Court, it was found to be very toothsome – somewhere between a chicken and a pheasant in flavour and texture. To prepare it for the kitchen, the Tudor cooks first cut its throat and hung it with a weight tied to its heels for two weeks in a cool place.[18] Turkeys were also available at this period: they were brought into Europe from Mexico and Central America about 1523–4, and into England at about the same time by the Strickland family of Boynton near Bridlington in the East Riding. The crest adopted by the Stricklands for their coat of arms showed a white turkey cock with a black beak and red wattles – probably representing the colouring of those early birds. Listed as one of the greater fowls by Archbishop Cranmer in 1541, the turkey soon gained an excellent reputation, being 'very good nourishment; restoreth bodily forces; passing good for such as are in recovery; maketh store of seede; enflameth Venus'. For preparation, they were simply hung overnight and cooked quite fresh.[19]

Using money advanced to them by the clerk for the coming month, the Hampton Court purveyors would purchase their poultry as required. In the case of shortages, they could compulsorily requisition supplies from members of the Poulterers' Company of London, paying the agreed prices. The Company was also obliged to buy back at the same rates any supplies that the palace purveyors found they didn't need. In return for these impositions, it was agreed that the purveyors would not take any poultry from within seven miles of London, and that they would not purchase any birds offered to them by nobles or gentlemen.[20] Most of the poultry was probably unloaded in the poultry yard so as to be ready for preparation before five in the morning.[21] The sergeant then checked it for quality and quantity.[22] If it contained any bad stuff, he rejected it and reported the purveyor to the clerks of the greencloth for punishment, while if it was of overall poor quality he could call in the clerks comptroller, who would reduce the price accordingly. As soon as it was accepted, the poultry was carried into the scalding house, where great pans of water would already be boiling over the fires. If the birds were dipped in for half a minute, the feathers could easily be plucked out by pulling them against the grain.[23] Since this process heated the carcases, it could make them go off within a day. Long experience had made this common knowledge, so the birds were plucked immediately before being cooked; those for late-morning dinner were delivered fresh to the larder by 8 a.m., and those for early-evening supper by 3 p.m. They were probably delivered drawn, but with their heads and feet in place to make it easier to tie them on to the spit, and with their major organs still inside for use by the cooks in specific recipes.

To the east of the Poultry, in the centre of the outer offices, lay the bakehouse.[24] At Hampton Court at this time the sergeant of the bakehouse was John Heath. He it was who had provided all the 'hard tack' biscuits for the King's siege of Boulogne in July 1544, and personally served there as a standard-bearer in the army, for which he earned an additional two shillings a day. Assisted by his clerk, he supervised the provision of all the bread required for the court.[25] The supplies of wheat were either purchased from outside or brought in from the royal estates by two yeomen purveyors, each load being delivered by cart or by barge and then measured by the bushel (64 pints, 36 litres); the sergeant or his clerk would always ensure that all of it was sweet and good for baking.[26] Some of the six 'conducts' (labourers) would carry it up the two broad staircases from the yard into the granaries, where the yeoman garnetor cleaned it and turned it, as necessary, to prevent it being spoiled by mildew or pests. This officer was also responsible for sending the wheat to be ground at the mills; he would make sure to check that the same weight that went out as grain returned as meal, for the King never surrendered a percentage of the meal as toll, but paid for the miller's services in cash.

On its return, the meal was boulted, or sieved, by the labourers. A coarse sieve first removed the bran, which the sergeant sold to the avener for feeding the King's horses. The remaining meal was either used to make 'cheat', or wheatmeal bread, or put through a very fine sieve to produce an almost white 'mayne' flour for making small loaves of the highest quality, called manchets. For general use the yeoman fernour (a baker in charge of the ovens or furnaces) would season the flour, prepare the leaven or yeast, make sure the dough was not too wet, check its weight in his balance both before and after baking, and heat the ovens in the great bakehouse. John Wynkell, the yeoman baker for the King's mouth, made the 'mayne, chete and payne de [bread of] mayne' for the royal table quite separately in the privy bakehouse. In 1546 the King had granted him the additional office of bailiff and collector of revenues for the lands of dissolved Leicester Abbey, in both Leicestershire and Derbyshire.[27]

The bulk of the Bakehouse's production was the cheat bread, the wholemeal loaves that in 1472 are recorded as weighing about 1lb 9oz (725g) each.[28] Around 200 or more messes of cheat were required every day to serve with meals, along with a minimum of 150 additional loaves to provide the breakfast, afternoon and supper-time snacks for those who had bouche of court. Similarly, over 700 manchets were required for the upper household's meals, and further supplies for bouche-of-court staff.

To make the cheat bread, the wholewheat flour was tipped into a deep wooden dough trough, and a hole scooped in the middle. Into this was poured a solution of old sourdough mixed with lukewarm water; next, it was mixed until it thickened enough to resemble pancake batter, as Gervase Markham tells us in his *The English Hus-wife* of 1615.[29] The batter was then covered with more meal and left to ferment overnight to form a spongy mass. In the morning, the remaining meal was kneaded in with a little warm water, yeast and salt to form a dough. Kneading by hand was far too laborious and slow for operations of this scale, and so it would either have been worked beneath a 'brake', a long beam secured to a bench by means of a strong iron shackle, or folded into a large clean cloth and trodden under foot. It is possible that the canvas 'couch cloths' (table cloths) purchased for the Bakehouse in the 1540s were used for this purpose.[30] Having been left to rise for a while the dough was then divided into individual loaves, which were weighed, worked or moulded into shape, and left to rise once more, ready for baking in the ovens.

CHEAT BREAD

Since the original sourdough method is inconvenient for modern domestic use, this following recipe uses fresh or dried yeast but retains the old method of setting the sponge.

800lb (1lb 12oz) wholewheat flour
10ml (2 tsp) salt
water at blood heat
15g (½oz) fresh yeast or its equivalent of prepared dried yeast

1. *Mix the flour and salt in a warm bowl, then scoop a hollow in the centre, leaving a thick layer across the base.*
2. *Dissolve the yeast in 425ml (¾ pt) water in a jug, then pour this slowly into the hollow in the flour, stirring continuously to form a smooth batter. Try to stir the batter only, without working in too much of the flour.*
3. *Cover the batter with some of the dry flour from the sides of the*

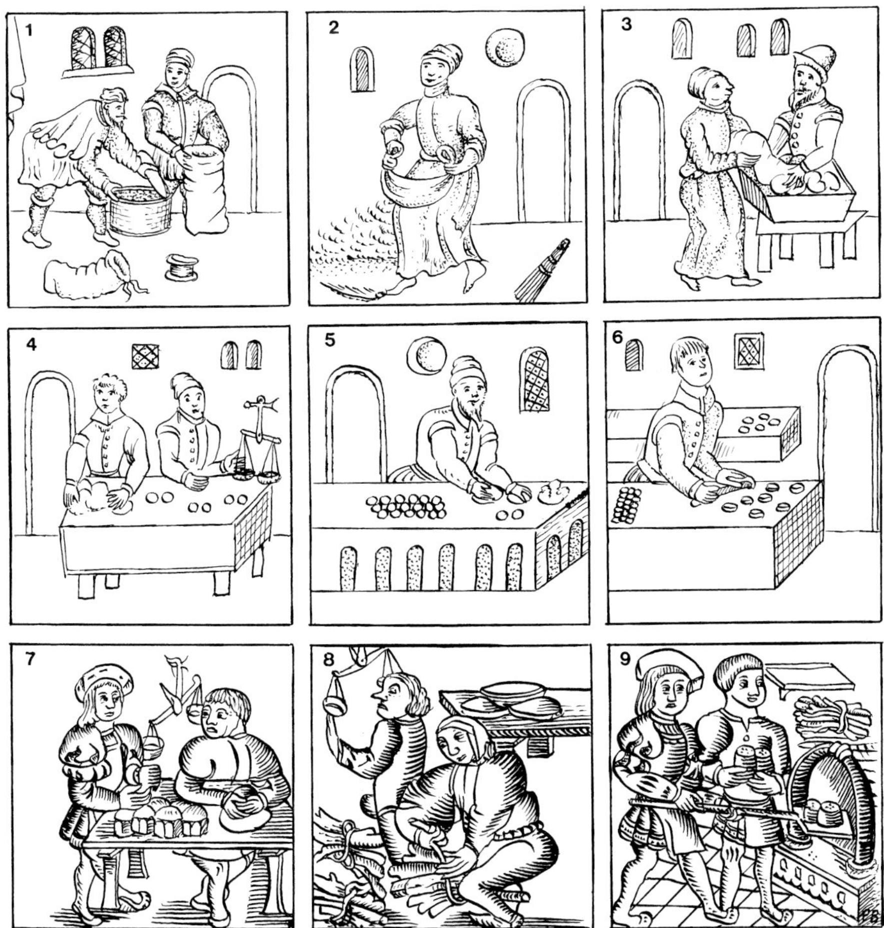

4. *Tudor breadmaking* These drawings based on the 1596 ordinances of the York Bakers' Company and on a mid sixteenth century assize of bread (bottom row) show the processes which the bakers and their labourers would have carried out here:

1. Measuring the wheat on its arrival, using a bushel measure and a 'strike' to level its surface.
2. Boulting the ground meal through a piece of canvas to remove the bran. Note the goose-wing and the brush for sweeping up the flour.
3. Mixing the dough in a trough.
4. Weighing manchet dough.
5. Moulding manchet loaves.
6. Cutting the manchets around the sides with a knife.
7. Moulding cheat loaves.
8. Tying up faggots for the oven. This labourer is wearing a linen coif, a close-fitting cap tied beneath the chin, to keep his head clean and warm.
9. Setting the bread into the oven.

bowl, place a light cloth over the top, and leave it in a warm place to ferment for an hour.
4. *Pour a further 150ml (¼ pt) of the water into the batter, then begin to mix the batter into the rest of the flour to form a dough, adding a little more water if necessary (different flours have different rates of absorption). Then knead the dough for 10 minutes, cover it with the cloth and leave it to rise in a warm place for about an hour.*
5. *Turn the dough out on to a floured board, knead it for 2–3 minutes, then divide it into two, forming each half into a round loaf. Place on a lightly greased baking sheet, cover with the cloth, and keep in the warm for 30 minutes or more, until doubled in size.*
6. *Pre-heat the oven to 230°C (450°F, gas mark 8) and bake for 30–35 minutes.*

To make manchet bread, fine boulted white flour would be similarly tipped into the dough trough and have a hollow scooped out of it, but instead of sourdough, a barm or liquid ale-yeast would be poured in – the sergeant purchasing this as required.[31] Having been mixed with salt and warm water, it was kneaded up on the brake or under foot, allowed to rise, then kneaded once more and divided up into individual loaves or rolls. Once each loaf had been weighed and shaped into a smooth ball, it was lightly rotated with the left hand while a knife in the right would slash it all the way round. A stick or a finger was then used to poke a dimple into it from top to bottom. This preparation gave the manchets their characteristic shape and quality. With the sides of the loaf slashed, the dough was free to rise upwards, giving a lighter, taller end product, much better for table use and also occupying less of the valuable oven space. The dimple, meanwhile, prevented the fermentation gases from forming unwelcome bubbles under the upper crust.

MANCHETS

900g (2lb) unbleached white flour
10ml (2 tsp) salt
water at blood heat
25g (1oz) fresh yeast, or its equivalent of prepared dried yeast

1. *Mix the flour and salt in a warm bowl, and scoop a hollow in the top.*
2. *Dissolve the yeast in 575ml (1pt) of the water, pour this into the flour, mix it in, then knead it thoroughly for 10 minutes. Cover it with*

a light cloth and leave it to rise in a warm place for 1–1½ hours.
3. Turn the dough out on to a floured board, knead it for 2–3 minutes, then divide it into six loaves.
4. Form each loaf into a ball and make a 7mm (¼in) cut all round it, then use the index finger or the handle of a wooden spoon to make a dimple from top to bottom through the middle of the loaf.
5. Place the loaves on lightly greased baking sheets 5–8cm (2–3in) apart, cover with the cloth, and leave in a warm place for 30 minutes or more until doubled in size.
6. Pre-heat the oven to 230°C (450°F, gas mark 8) and bake for 15–20 minutes, until well risen and a pale golden-brown.

The ovens used both in the bakehouses and in the main kitchens were of the traditional wood-fired kind. To house each oven, tons of insulating sand and rubble were encased within the brick walls of the bakehouses. Inside this mass, the large, flat circular floor of each brick-built oven was surrounded by a low wall, which supported a shallow dome of tiles set edge to edge to form a fireproof chamber. The only entrance was by a doorway at one side – the lintel of which was often pierced by a flue to carry away the smoke and steam from inside, but for the largest ovens in the palace kitchens this was replaced by a huge smoke-hood. To heat the oven, bundles of light branches were used, dry hawthorn being particularly good for this purpose because when 'bound into faggots . . . and burnt in ovens and in furnaces . . . they be soon kindled in the fire, and give a strong light, and sparkleth, and cracketh, and maketh much noise, and soon after they be brought all to nought'.[32] This kind of fuel, in the quantities needed by the palaces, cost £40 a year in the 1540s.[33]

Having been set alight, probably by being held over an open fire at the end of a long iron oven-fork, the flaming faggots would be either placed to one side or scattered over the oven floor and allowed to burn out, their flames licking the roof of the oven as they reached towards the open door. Once the brick structure had absorbed sufficient heat, sparks would fly at the mere rubbing of a twig across its dome; a little flour sprinkled on its floor would quickly turn dark brown, but not burst into flame. The bakers may then have taken a long iron bar with an L-shaped end, called a rooker, to rake out most of the ashes, and they would certainly have used a hoe, a semi-circular blade on the end of a long handle, to remove most of the remaining ashes and loose dust. They would then have dipped a long mop called a mawkin into a tub of water and swabbed out the final ashes, thereby introducing a degree of moisture into the oven before inserting the bread.

5. *Tudor bread* A cheat loaf of coarse wheatmeal flour, and a manchet of fine unbleached white flour, showing its characteristic dimple on the top and encircling slash.

The fully risen loaves, probably arranged on broad planks or work-boards, were then brought to the oven; each one would be scooped up on to the spade-shaped blade of an oven peel and skilfully set in place within the oven's dark interior. Now the oven door, probably made of sheet iron, was propped in place and its edges cemented with thick mud or clay, thus totally sealing the new batch until it had finished cooking. Only then was the door removed and the loaves taken out with the peel to cool, finally to be placed in the bread room for storage. Freshly baked bread was considered very unhealthy, all those who enjoyed its fine taste and texture fully expecting soon to be suffering from painful heartburn. As Dr Andrew Boorde advised:

> Hote breade is unholsom for any man, for it doth lye in the stomacke lyke a sponge, haustyng undecoct humours [causing indigestion]; yet the smell of newe breade is comfortable to the heade and to the harte. [Bread must be] a daye & a nyght olde, nor it is not good when it is past 4 or 5 dayes olde, except the loves [loaves] be great . . . Olde bread or stale bread doth drye up the blode or naturall moyster of man, & it doth engender evyll humours, and it is evyll and tarde of dygectyon [slowly digested].[34]

From the bread store, the clerk of the bakery recorded its distribution to the various offices that would use it. Most went to the Pantry, for the direct use of the household, while smaller quantities went to the Wafery and the Saucery to be used as ingredients in their products. Each day 102 loaves were also sold to the officers of the leash for a farthing each, for feeding the King's greyhounds.[35]

✿

The third part of the outer offices, nearest to the palace, was occupied by the Woodyard.[36] This came under the responsibility of John Gwyllim, the sergeant of the woodyard. In addition to his wages, Gwyllim enjoyed a considerable income from grants made to him by the King. These included the lease of prize wines, and the collection of custom duties as well as the subsidy of taxes and duties from the port and town of Bristol, and the lease of four former Whitefriar's tenements near St Dunstan's in Fleet Street, London. He also undertook the unlikely role of purveyor, buying hops and stockfish worth some £335 for Calais and Boulogne in 1545.[37] He and his clerk supervised the delivery of wood and rushes for the court, following the same accounting procedures as those described for the Bakehouse. In the 1540s they were supplying:[38]

in Wood for fewell, over and above Bouche of Court	£440		
in Rushes and straw, by estimacion	£60		
in necessaries, as Planks, Boords, quarter of Boords, Tressells, Formes, Cupboards, with Carpenters hyred	£10		
th'expences of Purveyors and other officers	£6	13	4d
	£516	13	4d

The fuel listed here, used to heat all the public rooms in the palace as well as to maintain all the fires in the kitchens, consisted of faggots, which were made from the smaller branches so burned fairly quickly, and talshides, timbers of a more substantial size that could maintain the fires throughout the day. Because trees and branches do not come in standard sizes, a quick and efficient method of measuring them had to be developed so that they could be fairly distributed according to the ordinances. Each log appears to have been about four feet (1.2m) in length and classified by its cross-section, as determined by measuring its girth according to a system which was later formalised by Queen Elizabeth.[39] The smallest size – for example a number one talshide, could either be a complete log of about sixteen inches' (40cm) girth and about five inches' (13cm) diameter, or of nineteen inches' (48cm) girth when split down the middle lengthways from a seven-and-a-half-inch (18.5cm) diameter log, or eighteen and a half inches' (47cm) girth when quarter-split from a ten-inch (25cm) diameter

6. *Bread and pastry ovens* This detail based on the painting of *The Field of the Cloth of Gold* (c. 1545) shows Henry VIII's bakehouse or pastry staff operating a bank of ovens using (1) a hoe to scrape the ashes out of the ovens, (2) mawkins to mop them out, (3) peels for putting the food in the ovens and taking it out, (4) iron oven doors and (5) a tub, probably to hold the clay for sealing the doors.

log. There was then a sliding scale extending up to a size seven; the first four sizes would be:

Size	*Complete log*	*Half-split*	*Quarter-split*
1	16in (40cm)	19in (48cm)	18½in (47cm)
2	23in (58cm)	27in (68.5cm)	26in (66cm)
3	28in (71cm)	33in (84cm)	32in (81cm)
4	33in (84cm)	39in (99cm)	38in (96.5cm)

In this way the volume and burning capacity of each log could be readily measured for purchasing and accounting purposes, and also for meeting the needs of the particular users. In addition, faggots and talshides were supplied to all those who had bouche of court: dukes were allowed eight faggots and ten talshides per day; bishops, senior nobles, the Lords Chamberlain and Privy Seal, the Queen's maids and the Counting House, six faggots and eight talshides each; knights and senior members of the household staff, four of each; the Wardrobe and household officers, two of each; and the sergeants and gentlemen officers, one of each. Altogether, at least 400 faggots and a similar number of talshides would have been distributed around the palace on each winter's day.[40] The numerous smoking chimneys must have looked very impressive – the placing of the King's own apartments and gardens to the south-east of the palace, though, ensured that the prevailing south-west winds would keep them largely smoke-free.

As for the rushes, they would most probably have been the common rush, *Juncus*, whose clumps of tapering tubular green stems grow two feet (61cm) or more in height in most wet heaths and fields in this country. Their main use then was as a floor-covering. Even though many rooms in the palace were fitted with mats made of bulrushes – plaited into four-inch (10cm) strips, then stitched together to make them up to the required size, John Cradocke having obtained a lifetime monopoly in 1539 for supplying them to all the royal palaces within twenty miles of London – loose rushes continued to be strewn.[41] Writing to Wolsey's physician, Erasmus had described English floors as having accumulations of up to twenty years' rushes, stinking with the vilest mass of filth and rotting vegetable matter, but neither archaeology nor any contemporary evidence can confirm this.[42] Nicolò di Favri of the Venetian embassy more accurately observed: 'In England, over the floors they strew weeds called "rushes" which resemble reeds . . . Every eight or ten days they put down a fresh layer; the cost of each layer being half a Venetian livre, more or less, according to the size of the house.'[43]

To keep the rushes clean, the three grooms who were responsible for strewing them in Edward VI's Privy Chamber each morning had to sweep away all those that were matted, while the description of Queen Elizabeth's presence chamber strewn with rushes (which he mistook for straw) given by Paul Hentzner of Brandenburg, travelling tutor to a Silesian noble, and Ben Jonson's of 'ladies and gallants languishing upon the Rushes' show them to have been a clean and relatively high-status floor-covering.[44] Certainly, a monarch as fastidious as Henry VIII would never have allowed masses of stinking rushes to lie about his palace. In practice, the *Juncus* type of rushes provide a warm insulating layer, quiet to walk upon, and give any room a delightfully moist and piquant scent, as anyone knows who has attended the rush-bearing service in St Oswald's Church at Grasmere in the Lake District.[45] In addition, they help to contain the dust, grit, grease and small litter, leaving the floor quite clean when they are swept out with a broom, and so making them the ideal covering for rooms such as the Great Hall at Hampton Court.

Rushes were also used for other purposes. If their outer layer was peeled off, leaving only a narrow strip to support the fine spongy pith, they could be used as wicks for pricket candles or oil lamps. Henry's Privy Purse expenses included payments 'for a potell of salet [salad] oyle 2s 6d; for a bottell and for Rushes to brenne [burn] wt. the saied oyle 3d'; and if dipped in tallow, they formed rush lights and tapers.[46] Dry rushes could be used to light fires or lanterns, or even to make pallets or mattresses for servants.[47] A number of junior officers, such as the under-clerk comptroller, were provided with 'lytter and rushes for [their] paylette', while Henry VII's household regulations include instructions for shaking up a layer of litter – suggesting the manner in which the rushes may have been prepared for the purpose – and laying it between two layers of canvas to form a base for his feather bed.

Running parallel to the river, at the back of the Woodyard, were the stables where the purveyors of the Poultry, the Bakehouse and the Woodyard could keep their horses. By the 1880s these stables had fallen into ruin and over the course of the following decades, along with every other building in this block, they were demolished and the whole area grassed over, leaving no visual evidence that a major domestic building had ever occupied the site.

4

The Greencloth Yard

Jewel House, Spicery, Chandlery

Virtually everyone concerned with the domestic management of Hampton Court, along with every item of its food, drink and fuel, had to enter the main palace buildings from the Outer Court by way of the Back Gate (no. 3). As they approached, they would be directly observed by the administrative staff working in the counting house up on the first floor of the gatehouse. At the gateway itself, once the great oak doors had been swung back, they would be challenged by one of the porters. This man was responsible to William Knevet, the sergeant porter who had served as a captain at the siege of Boulogne, and his job was to prevent

> any Vagabonds, Rascalls, or Boyes [entering] in at the Gate at any time; and that one of [the porters] shall three or four times in the day make due search through the House, in case that negligently at any time, any Boyes or Rascalls have escaped by them . . . and put them out again . . . the said Portes shall have vigilant eyes to the Gate, that they doe not permitt any kind of Victualls, Waxe-lights, Leather Potts, Vessels Silver or Pewter, Wood or Coales, passe out of the Gates, upon paine of losse of three dayes Wages to every of them as often as they offend therein.[1]

To enforce their authority, the porters carried their traditional porter's staff, and also had the use of a pair of small stocks, which were transported from palace to palace in the Greencloths' carriage.[2] They were probably based in the small room to the right of the Gate, beneath the staircase there (no. 4). From their doorway, not only could they check every person and vehicle entering and leaving the palace, but they could also watch the door of the jewel house only a few feet away, and by scanning the courtyards see anyone entering the boiling house door to gain access to the main kitchens.

✿

The four ground-floor rooms to the left of the gate were occupied by the Jewel House (no. 6). Considering the fabulous value of Henry VIII's gold, silver and bejewelled artefacts as well as his superb gemstones, this would appear to be a ludicrously insecure and exposed location. But in fact, all those really valuable items were kept in a far safer 'secret' jewel house in the King's apartments, deep in the heart of the palace. This jewel house by the gate was used only to store the less valuable domestic pieces of gold, silver, coinage and so on. Although physically within the household offices, the Jewel House was administered quite independently, the master of the jewels being directly responsible to the King for all items placed in his care; he would issue and receive many whole and broken silver vessels as instructed by the Treasurer of the King's household, presumably including those intended for the use of the courtiers in the Great Chamber and other rooms of states.[3]

To perform these duties, the master of the jewels had two waiters, a clerk (and his servant), and a yeoman and a groom, who shared a servant. The yeoman and groom were particularly charged with the safety of the silver and so forth when it was in transit, the latter carrying the boxes to their department's 'charyet', or wagon, packing them and securely tying them down, and then, with the yeoman, guarding them as they were moved from one place to another. For such moves, smaller items and boxes were packed into great leather-covered iron-bound strongboxes called standards. Just before Candlemas on 2 February 1530, Henry had sent 'three or four cartloads of stuff, the most part lokked in great standerds', to the disgraced Wolsey at nearby Esher; then just a few months later, on 11 May, he purchased two more standards for £3 1s 8d to carry quantities of gold and silver plate from York Place, the Cardinal's former London residence as Archbishop of York, back to Hampton Court.[4]

✿

Beyond the archway of the Back Gate, the walls fall back to each side, to provide convenient 'parking bays' for carts and so on unloading their goods into the stores and offices which lined this first courtyard, the Greencloth Yard (no. 11). Proceeding down the left, or north, side of the yard, the first door in the corner gave access to a spiral stair leading up to the comptroller's lodgings, while the second led into the jewel house. The next two doorways, each with a narrow window to one side, were the entrances to the Comptroller's cellar and the King's coal house (nos 9 and 10), constructed within the area of the moat, which ran through this area up to 1530.

At this period the word 'coal' was used to describe both the charcoal made by baking wood in kilns and the 'sea-coal' dug out of the ground. It is probable that the 'Coals in the year, by estimacion £324', purchased by the Scullery and Woodyard were charcoal, used in cooking stoves, in small portable dish-warmers called chafing-dishes and in small portable room-heaters called stoves.[5] In the 1540s the 'coal' was delivered by the 'quarter', a measure of eight bushels (about 290 litres) and was probably stored in the cellars here until required by the various kitchen offices or by the King, the Queen or Princess Mary – courtiers were not provided with any supplies to heat their rooms.[6] For the King's Chamber, it was put in baskets containing one third of a quarter, some three and a half cubic feet (0.1 cubic metres); each basket would be checked for volume and then marked by the clerks comptroller.[7] This 'coal' was probably charcoal: if it had been sea-coal it would have weighed around two hundredweight (100kg), and would have been too heavy for the groom porters to conveniently carry up to the chambers. It is also notable that none of Henry VIII's fireplaces were provided with the iron grates that were essential for coal fires.

If sea-coal was used at Hampton Court at this time, as suggested by a layer of coal excavated from the cellars in 1984, it is far more likely to have been used to fuel the large room-heating stoves.[8] Introduced from the Continent, these had their fireboxes and flues clad with finely moulded glazed earthenware tiles, to work rather like giant storage radiators. One of these was certainly in use at Whitehall (formerly Cardinal Wolsey's residence, then known as York Place), where green-glazed tiles bearing the initials 'HR' were excavated from the bathroom area in the 1930s, and there was probably a similar example at Hampton Court. When Baron Waldstein visited the palace in 1600, he found that 'In the Queen's bathroom there is a stove, and in its upper part a certain metal which the English call by the extraordinary name of sea-coal; by heating this the room itself is warmed.'[9]

Returning to the Back Gate, we now go along the right, or south side of the Greencloth Yard. In the corner by the Gatehouse were two doorways: the first was the staircase to the counting house, up to which the White Sticks, the clerks of the kitchen and spicery, the purveyors and others would

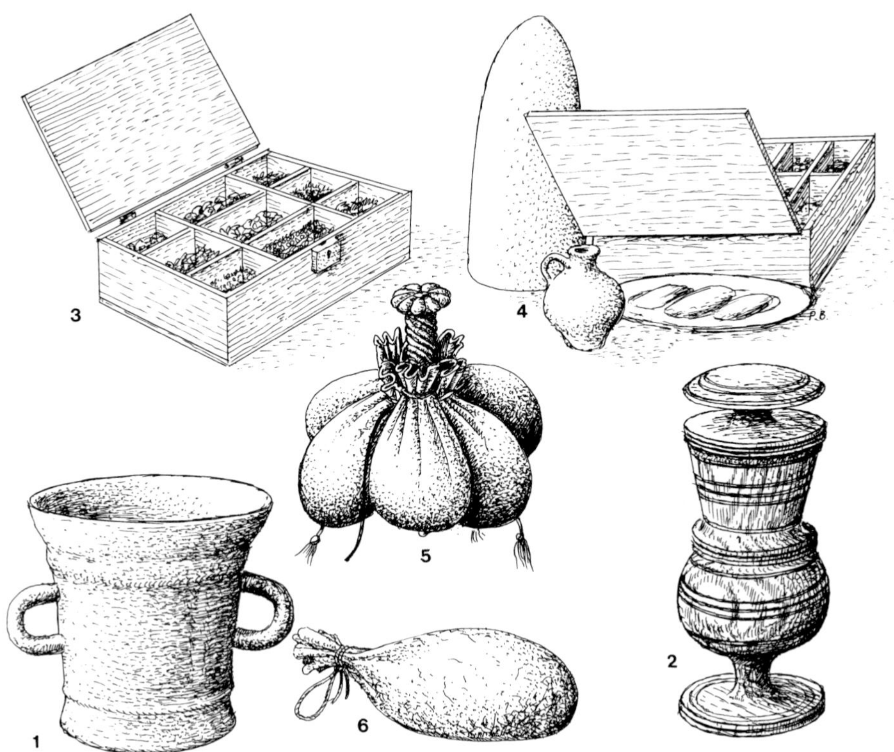

7. *Spicery Equipment* These drawings, based on contemporary illustrations, show (1) a bronze mortar for reducing the spices to a fine powder and (2) a mortar mill in which the spices were grated between iron plates and would then collect in the lower bulbous section. The lockable wooden spice-boxes (3 and 4) ensured that their expensive contents were kept secure in the kitchen. The ground spices were hung up in the spice-purse with its leather bags (5), or in bladders (6), ready for use.

have passed on their way up to the greencloth, while the second led into the counting house's ground-floor room. Next, half-way along the wall, came the door into the spicery office (no. 12), where the chief clerk of the Spicery supervised not only the spicery office itself but also those of the Chandlery, the Confectionary, the Ewery, the Wafery and the Laundry. Within five days of each month's end, this clerk had to make a list, or 'parcel', of all the provisions he had bought in, noting any sales on the back of the list and then passing it to the cofferer together with any money received.[10] In addition, he had to complete his annual returns to the Greencloth within two months of the year's end, or else be fined three months' wages.

As far as the spices were concerned, these included all the popular medicinal and flavouring ingredients of the period. Andrew Boorde listed the most common as ginger, pepper, nutmeg, mace, cloves, cinnamon, saffron, liquorice, grains of Paradise (the seeds of *Aframomum melegueta*, a West African plant of the ginger family) and galingale (another spice similar to ginger) to which may be added caraway, aniseed and coriander.[11] Some of these were distributed to the kitchens, the saucery and the confectionary in their whole form, but if required as a powder they were ground by William Hutchinson, the yeoman of the spicery, probably using a bell-metal or marble mortar, and sieved to ensure that they were of sufficient fineness.[12] Some indication of the furniture and equipment he may have used may be gathered from the 1599 inventory of the spice house of Sir Thomas Ramsey, Lord Mayor of London:[13]

Itm. an iron beame and skales . . .		10s	
Itm. two brasse morters wayinge 164lb (74kg] net at 4d ob [ha'penny]	£3	1s	6d
Itm. two olde presses			
Itm. an olde counter			
Itm. two small paire of balance . . .			
Itm. two boxes, 3 barrells . . .			
Itm. 3 spice treyes . . .			
Itm. two piles of brasen waghts poize [weight] 31lb [14kg] at 4d ob		12s	
Itm. browne paper, and white in the cupboard . . .		3s	

The Spicery also dealt with items we would not now describe as spices, such as dates, figs, raisins and other dried fruits, sugar and other groceries, as well as fresh fruits such as the apples, pears, quinces, oranges and lemons used by the household.[14]

Next door lay the chandlery (no. 13), where the clerk of the spicery maintained records of how much wax was brought in every day, and how much of it was distributed as candles and so on both for general household use and, weekly, to those who received such items as part of their bouche of court. According to the Black Book of 1472, the sergeant of the chandlery used both large and small balances, weights, pans, a travelling trunk, hot irons, and a 'carriage' and a pack-horse to carry the long coffers containing the lights of all sizes – in short, everything required to make and distribute torches and candles as needed.[15] To do this he was assisted by three yeomen. The first deputised for him in lighting the King's chamber and presenting the expenses for these lights to the ushers there. The second yeoman had to help make the lights and distribute them to each person according to their bouche of court entitlement, and then supervise two grooms to collect all the unburnt pieces of the larger lights from every lodging in the palace by nine each morning. The third yeoman, 'cunnynge in waxemakinge', assisted them in these tasks, and also supervised the lights in the Great Hall and chambers. Finally there was a page who did all the dirty and unskilled work such as cleaning the Chandlery, fetching the wood and charcoal, and carrying equipment and stores to and from the wagon whenever the court was on the move.

Most of the lights were made of beeswax, which at £400 a year, not including the bouche-of-court supplies, was extremely expensive.[16] The largest lights were torches. These were made by dipping lengths of tow, coarse hemp or flax fibres or fine linen rags into the wax and rolling them to form columns probably some three feet (90cm) long and around three-quarters of an inch (2cm) in diameter. A number of these, perhaps six, would then be waxed together around the top of a wooden shaft to form a torch. Such costly lights were provided only for the King, the nobles and the highest officials.[17] Links (a shorter kind of torch) were made in a similar manner, but instead of being mounted on an integral shaft they were spiked on portable iron cressets mounted on long poles; Henry VIII's inventory listed 1000lb (454kg) of links for cressets, plus twenty cressets, in one of his stores.[18]

To light the King's chambers, square blocks of wax with a central wick were used, 14lb (6.3kg) of fine wax being purchased to make these 'quarriers' for the King in 1531.[19] They were delivered from the chandlery every day, and their remains, along with the ends of the torches, were collected by the grooms of the chamber who passed them to the groom porters for return to the chandlery for remelting.[20]

For general good-quality lighting, the senior members of the court used one pricket candle every winter's day. This consisted of a peeled rush or a plaited wick over which warm wax was poured until it was probably an inch (2.5cm) or more in diameter, so that it could be stuck on to the spike of either a wall-mounted or a portable pricket candlestick.[21] Smaller candles made in the same way were called sizes, most courtiers and household officers receiving two of these each day in winter. The cheapest candles used at the palace were called white lights. These were distributed by weight, a duke receiving a pound (450g) a day, for example, and each courtier and upper household servant eight ounces (225g). In the late fifteenth century the royal household was still using pieces of bread to hold the smaller candles; the first yeoman of the chandlery would draw loaves from the Pantry for this particular use in the King's Chamber, later returning those that remained unused.[22] Henry VII's 'grand porter' had kept a

8. *Tudor Lighting* The Chandlery made the long beeswax torches (1) used only for the royal family and nobles (shown in BM Add MS 24098); the shorter 'link' (2) was mounted on a long pole for more general use. It also made the candles for wooden lanterns (3), pricket candlesticks (4) and socket candlesticks (5), as well as quarriers (6) – the large square night-lights used for the King's Privy Chambers and other royal rooms.

ladder near the Great Chamber 'redie to sett upp sises withall on a plate; which plate ought to be hanged on the uppermost side of the arras' at frieze level.[23] By the sixteenth century candlesticks with sockets were already in regular use; 'two Candlesticks of silver gilt with sockettes' weighing over twenty-four ounces (700g) were recorded at Hampton Court in 1547, for example.[24]

Beyond the chandlery, in the corner of the Greencloth Yard on the south side of the inner gateway, a doorway led into the rooms of the clerk comptroller (no. 15). Just opposite, and entered from the gate passage, is a room identified in the 1674 inventory as the Bottle House, but its use in the 1540s is uncertain (no. 17). In 1545 the groom of the bottles was John Mawde, to whom the King had granted the lease of the watermills at Carleton and Burton in Yorkshire.[25] Mawde was responsible to the sergeant of the cellar for carrying wine in large leather bottles slung from the sides of his bottle-horse, and for ensuring that none was lost or dispensed along the way. Since the storage of beer and wine in glass bottles only began on a large scale in the Elizabethan and Stuart periods, there would appear to have been little need for a bottle house in the palace in the 1540s, and this room probably had another use when first built. It may well have been associated with the adjacent dry fish house and salt store, with which it communicated directly by means of an internal door. Certainly there would have been a great need for such a cool, dark store with no south-facing windows to keep supplies of salt beef, especially during the winter months.

Salt beef formed an important part of the diet of virtually every Tudor household, and it enjoyed a sound reputation. Andrew Boorde wrote:

> Beef is good meat for an Englishman so be it the meat be young; for old beef and cow-flesh doth engender melancholy and leprous humours. If it be moderately powdered [salted], that the gross blood by salt may be exhausted, it doth make an Englishman strong, the education of him with it considered. Martylmas beef, which is called 'hang beef' in the roof of the smoky house is not laudable. It may fill the belly, and cause a man to drink, but it is evil for the [kidney-] stone, and of evil digestion, and maketh no good juice.[26]

Salt beef was usually prepared around Martinmas, 11 November, when the cattle were still in good condition after their summer grazing and before they had to be fed on expensive hay and peas. As Thomas Tusser, in his *Five Hundred Points of Good Husbandry* (1577), advised:[27]

> November [for Easter] at Martilmas, hang up a beef,
> For stall-fed and pease-fed, play pickpurse the thief.
> With that and the like, ere grass-beef come in,
> Thy folk shall look cheerly, when others look thin.

The first task when salting beef was to decide whether it was to be dry-salted or wet-salted. The first method involved rubbing a mixture of common salt, bay salt (a salt with large crystals made by evaporating sea-water by the heat of the sun in the Bay of Biscay), saltpetre (potassium nitrate) and coarse brown sugar into the meat. Plain salt would have tended to dry out the surface of the beef, making it as hard as a board, but mixing it with saltpetre helped the salt to penetrate and gave the beef an appetising pink colour, while the sugar softened it and so counteracted the hardening effects of the salt. As with most everyday processes, the methods of salting were almost never written down, since everyone knew them by heart and experience, and had no need to refer to a book to remind them what to do. Later cookery books, and the practices of country people of the present generation, all indicate that it was a very straightforward process, as this traditional recipe shows:[28]

DRY-SALT OR CORNED BEEF

1800g (4lb) brisket of beef	225g (8oz) sea salt
50g (2oz) dark-brown sugar	15g (½oz) saltpetre

1. Place the meat in a deep dish, rub in the sugar for 10–15 minutes, and leave in a cold place overnight. Then rub it again and leave it a second night.
2. Rub in the salt and saltpetre, turning and rubbing the meat for 10–15 minutes each day for another four days.
3. Rinse the meat, form it into a roll, and tie it in place with tape.
4. Put it into a pan of cold water, cover, slowly bring it to the boil, then skim off any scum and reduce the heat to a very gentle simmer for a further 2–2½ hours, skimming as necessary.
5. Drain the meat and either serve it hot, in which case prepared cabbage, carrots or similar vegetables may be put in with it 30 minutes before serving; or press the meat overnight and serve cold.

When large quantities of salt beef were being prepared, this rubbing and turning process was frequently replaced by wet-salting, for which the meat had only to be soaked in a brine probably prepared as follows:[29]

WET-SALT BEEF

1800g (4lb) brisket of beef	15ml (1tbs) coarse sea salt
40g (1½oz) saltpetre	225g (8oz) coarse brown sugar
250g (9oz) common salt	2.3l (4pt) hot water

1. Put the salts and sugar into a large pot, and scald this with the hot water. Stir it, and leave it until all has dissolved and it is quite cold.
2. Put in the beef, ensuring that it is covered, and leave it for 2–3 days, turning it every day. For modern use, this is sufficient to give it the characteristic salt-beef taste, but traditionally it was stored in this brine for two or three months.
3. Remove the beef from the brine, rinse, and follow points 3 to 5 in the dry-salt recipe.

Wet-salting was certainly carried out at Hampton Court – the palace was provided with 'ranges for the cawdren to stand upon for the seething and boiling of bryne for the larder'.[30] The beef was first cut up into pieces weighing 2lb (900g) each, which was enough for one mess for four people, and then immersed in the brine as described above, until it was completely impregnated. During this process the salt made it shrink, but, as the Privy Council informed Lord Hertford when he was mounting the 1544 expedition against Scotland, even if this caused the meat to weigh less, it still contained 'as much feeding, and more, than two pounds of fresh beef' when it had been soaked and boiled ready for the table. For storage, the beef was packed into 'pipes', large wooden casks of 105 gallons (about 478 litres) capacity, each of which held four hundred pieces, enough to provide 1,600 individual servings.[31]

5

The Pastry Yard

Saucery, Confectionary, Pastry

From the inner gateway, the Pastry Yard looks almost square (no. 19). It is surrounded on the north, east and west sides by Henry VIII's kitchen offices of 1530–2, while to the south the earlier lodgings of Wolsey's Base Court extend away eastwards, leaving a wide, open paved passage leading up towards the Great Hall.

This passage was essential for allowing daylight into the lodgings, but it also provided an effective firebreak between the kitchen offices and the main residential part of the palace. More importantly, it provided a direct route for carting such items as barrels of beer down to the cellars beneath the Great Hall and for the bread bearers to carry the manchet and cheat loaves from the bakehouse to the bread room near the buttery; the passage would also have been used to bring the talshides and faggots from the woodyard to feed the palace's numerous fires, and the torches, links and candles from the chandlery to provide its illumination. As the main service passage, it must have been a constantly busy thoroughfare, its security ensured by being under constant surveillance from the clerk comptroller's rooms.

Starting from the inner gateway and proceeding clockwise around the yard, the first door led via a staircase to the offices of the clerk of the kitchen, directly over the gateway, and to those of the Scullery (no. 20), where the sergeant and two clerks of the scullery and woodyard kept their accounts. The next door gave access to the fish larder, described in the building accounts as the dry fish house (no. 18).[1] As fish was the main fasting-day food, eaten every Friday and Saturday and throughout Lent, it was important that the palace always had supplies ready to hand, and so they followed Thomas Tusser's advice:[2]

9. *Ling* This large variety of cod formed the bulk of the salt-fish eaten at Hampton Court.

When harvest is ended, take shipping or ride,
Ling, salt-fish and herring, for lent to provide;
To buy it at first, as it cometh to road
Shall pay for its charges thou spendest abroad.

Choose skilfully salt-fish, not burnt at the stone.
Buy such as be good, or else let it alone;
Get home that is bought, and go stack it up dry,
With peas-straw between it, the safer to lie

— for, Tusser continued, 'Dank Ling forgot, Will quickly rot.' Purchases of fish were made by the clerks comptroller and the sergeant of the acatery, probably with his clerk and John Hopkins, yeoman purveyor of sea-fish.[3] In Elizabeth's reign these officers were responsible for providing all the 'ling, coddes, stock-fish, salt-herring, salmon, salt eeles, grey-salt and white-salt' kept in store in the dry fish house, the yeoman of the salt store delivering them to the main kitchens and larders as required.[4] It made good sense to store the 'Bay Salt . . . £20' and 'White Salt £13 6 8d' here in the dry, for they would have deteriorated rapidly in the steamy boiling house and damp wet larders.[5]

For the King's and Queen's own use there were salt eel, salt lamprey, salt salmon and 'organ ling'.[6] The latter was the best kind of ling and the largest were caught around Orkney; one writer in 1603 described a superior person as 'Differing as much from other people . . . as Stockfishe or poor John from the large organe ling'.[7] Contemporary recipes give details of how these luxury foods were prepared for the table. The lamprey, the eel-like fish often caught in the Severn estuary that has a large, rasping sucker instead of jaws and no major bones except its spine, was soaked overnight in bran and water, then skinned, simmered with onions and served hot with a bread-and-vinegar sauce. Alternatively, it could have the loose salt dusted off and the spine removed, and was then soaked for a night and a day, scalded with straw or hay to enable the skin to be removed, and finally stewed with a dozen peeled onions. It was served cold with the onions minced into 'sauce camelyne',[8] (see p. 64). Calver salmon, meanwhile, could be eaten directly after being removed from its spiced brine, prepared as follows:[9]

TO CALVER SALMON

500g (1lb 2oz) salmon fillets or steaks
425ml (¾pt) white wine vinegar
275ml (½pt) white wine
10ml (2tsp) salt
2–3 pieces root ginger
2 sprigs rosemary
1 blade mace

1. *Simmer 150ml (¼pt) each of the vinegar and wine with the salt, spices and rosemary in a covered pan for 30 minutes.*
2. *Strain this liquid into a clean pan, and add the remaining vinegar and white wine. Bring it to the boil, put in the salmon, reduce the heat, and simmer gently for some 5 minutes, until just cooked. Each piece should be totally immersed as it cooks, so put them in in batches, as necessary.*
3. *Leave the salmon to cool in the liquid overnight, and eat within the next few days.*

For everyone else at court, however, the main salt-fish was ling, the largest variety of cod, which gave the best results when cooked. Much came into this country from Norway and Iceland, where, Andrew Boorde tells us, 'the people be good fyshers, much of theyr fyshe they do barter wyth English men, for mele [meal], lases [laces] and shoes'.[10] Quantities would be carried from the dry fish house into the wet larder a few days before each fish day, to soak there in tubs of water in readiness for cooking in the kitchens.

Next door to the dry fish house, a staircase went up to the first floor to a landing which led left into the pastry and saucery office (no. 21) and right into the confectionary (no. 22). The sergeant and clerk of the pastry, assisted by a yeoman, was responsible for the administration and accountancy of both the main pastry – where pies, pastries and tarts were baked – and the saucery. In the 1674 lodging list the Saucery is located in the hall-side dresser office, but although this is a large room it is unlikely that important officers such as the clerk of the kitchen and his companions would have wished to share their office with a mere yeoman, especially one who was constantly busy grinding, sieving and mixing various odoriferous ingredients, and so the saucery may well have been located elsewhere.

✿

The saucery concentrated on making the thick condiments eaten cold with the meat and fish, rather than the hot sauces made from the internal ingredients of the hot dishes cooked in the kitchens, although the yeoman of the saucery may have helped in their preparation by doing odd jobs such as grating bread. To make the sauces, the Saucery annually purchased 'in mustard, vinegar and vergeuice [an acid liquor obtained from sour fruit such as crab-apples] £50 . . . in herbs for sauces, by estimacion £4', as well as drawing supplies of bread from the Bakehouse, spices from the Spicery, and vinegar made by the Cellar from their 'feeble or dull wines'.[11]

The Saucery's most important product by far was mustard, which was 'bruised and ground with vinegar [as] a wholesome sauce, meet to be eaten with hard, gross meats, either flesh or fish'.[12] Henry Buttes, in his *Dyets Dry Dinner* of 1599, described it as 'Good sauce for sundrie meates, both flesh and fish; English Mustard; that is, much tart'.[13] First, the mustard seed was crushed, using either a pestle and mortar or perhaps a stone or iron ball in a bowl; then it was mixed with strong wine vinegar, strained into a pot, and tied down beneath a parchment cover until required for use. It could also be made sweeter – for pheasant, partridge or rabbit – or more powerful for the coarser meats.[14]

LOMBARD MUSTARD

60–90ml (4–6 tbs) white wine vinegar
30ml (2 tbs) honey
60ml (4 tbs) mustard powder

Mix the ingredients together, adding just enough vinegar to form a smooth sauce.

LADY HOLMEBY'S MUSTARD

60ml (4 tbs) mustard powder
60ml (4 tbs) dry sherry
20ml (4 tsp) sugar

Mix the ingredients together to form a smooth paste.

ROBERT MAY'S STRONG MUSTARD

150ml ($\frac{1}{4}$pt) white wine vinegar
1 large English onion
10ml (2 tsp) sugar
5ml (1 tsp) ground ginger
100g (4oz) mustard powder
2.5ml ($\frac{1}{2}$ tsp) white pepper
10ml (2 tsp) grated horseradish or horseradish sauce

1. Finely chop the peeled onion and soak it in the vinegar, with the horseradish, for 30 minutes. Then strain it through a sieve over a bowl, pushing it through with either the back of a spoon or the fingers, to extract all the juice. Discard the onion left in the sieve.
2. Mix in all the remaining ingredients.

This recipe gives a memorably powerful mustard, and should be used with caution by those unused to traditional mustards of the true English variety!
N.B. All these mustards may be sealed down in clean jars, and stored in a cool place ready for use.

Next in importance came greensauce, which was sometimes made with sorrel or gooseberries as in later periods, but also with herbs such as parsley and mint. It was especially recommended to accompany fresh fish such as halibut and turbot, for which it might be eaten along with mustard, since they went well together.[15]

GREENSAUCE

120ml (8 tbs) finely chopped fresh parsley
90ml (6 tbs) finely chopped fresh mint
1 clove fresh garlic, peeled and crushed
100g (4oz) fresh white bread crumbs
150ml ($\frac{1}{4}$pt) white wine vinegar
1.5ml ($\frac{1}{4}$ tsp salt)
pinch ground black pepper

Mix all the ingredients and liquidise to form a smooth paste, adding a little more vinegar if too thick.

For peacock, sauce ginger was recommended:[16]

SAUCE GINGER

100g (4oz) fresh white breadcrumbs
5–10ml (1–2 tsp) ground ginger
150ml (¼pt) white wine vinegar

Liquidise together to form a smooth paste.

For egret, plover, crane and bustard the best sauce was sauce camelyne, which took its name from 'canel' (cinnamon):[17]

SAUCE CAMELYNE

225g (8oz) white bread, sliced, toasted golden-brown, crusts removed
150ml (¼pt) white wine vinegar
150ml (¼pt) white wine
20ml (4 tsp) sugar
1.5ml (¼ tsp) ground cinnamon
1.5ml (¼ tsp) ground ginger
4ml (¾ tsp) ground cloves

Chop the toast into small cubes, soak it in the vinegar for 10 minutes, then liquidise it with the remaining ingredients.

✿

Across the landing from the saucery lay the confectionary – just a single room, but the one responsible for producing the most elaborate and expensive of all the foods prepared in the kitchen. At this period sugar was still a most expensive luxury food. First domesticated in New Guinea some ten thousand years earlier, it had entered the Roman world about the fifth century, and between the fourth and eighth centuries the Arabs had spread its cultivation around the Mediterranean. Northern Europeans first made contact with sugar during the first Crusade (1096–9), after which it began to be imported for the use of the English royal household, where 677lb (307kg) of plain sugar, 300lb (136kg) of violet sugar and 1,900lb (861kg) of rose sugar were being consumed in 1287. Columbus carried sugar-cane from the Canaries to the New World on his second voyage in 1493. The Spanish first cultivated it in San Domingo, using the labour of imported African slaves, and brought their first shipments back to Europe around 1516; they then went on to expand its production in their colonies in the Caribbean, Mexico and Paraguay, and along the Pacific coast of South

America. The Portuguese carried out a similar programme in Brazil, and were shipping sugar back to Lisbon by 1526. Although the sugar was refined to some extent in its country of origin, it was still too impure for high-quality use and so was further refined in northern Europe. Antwerp being the leading centre for this activity.

In early sixteenth century England sugar cost around 3d or 4d a pound (450g), but its growing popularity and scarcity saw it rise to 9d or 10d by 1544, when its price had to be checked by royal proclamation.[18] In the same year London established its first refinery. Here the sugar was dissolved and boiled in a lye of ashes or lime, the scum was skimmed off, and the syrup clarified with white of eggs. It was then placed in cone-shaped pottery moulds covered with a layer of wet clay, from which the water slowly dripped through the sugar, removing the remaining molasses. When this process was finished, the sugar cones were knocked out of their moulds and left in a warm room to dry out. The finished cones weighed anything from three to fourteen pounds (1.3–6.3kg) and were almost as hard and white as crystalline marble. It was not until 1551 that Captain Thomas Wyndham returned to England from Agudin, Morocco, with the first-ever cargo of sugar to be brought into this country by an English ship direct from its country of origin. The Tudor taste for sugar intensified so that the trade rapidly expanded, and by 1585 London had replaced Antwerp as the leading refinery centre in Europe.

Although the Spicery could acquire its sugar in good condition, it was very difficult to keep it that way because sugar readily absorbs moisture from the atmosphere and soon turns into an unpleasant sticky syrup. My own experience of Hampton Court's kitchens has brought this home to me: on one occasion, sugarwork that had dried to rock-hardness over some months began to dissolve and to weep syrup after only a day's exposure to the kitchens' damp winter air. Exhibiting great good sense and practicality, the architect who designed the kitchen offices placed the confectionary in the warmest and driest place in the whole palace – directly over the pastry ovens, a mass of some 80 cubic yards (61 cubic metres) of masonry that would have been continually fired up whenever the court was in residence. This constant source of dry underfloor heating made the confectionary ideal for sugarwork.

Most of the sugar, spices and dried fruits used in the Confectionary, along with some of the finished confectionery, was bought from one of the two Venetian galleys that used to arrive in Southampton each year, where one of them would unload and the other would keep its cargo intact for trading with Flanders on the return journey. The use of corporate hospitality to promote business was already a well established practice in the sixteenth century, and on one of these occasions the captain of the Venetian flag-galley provided the King and his court with a sumptuous entertainment. A large platform on the deck had been decorated with tapestry and silk, and on either side were four tables, each bearing dishes of every sort of confection for the three hundred guests. Henry passed down the centre and up to the poop deck, where he tasted sponge cakes and other sweetmeats, and the remainder was distributed among the nobles. Meanwhile, those at the tables below enjoyed their share of the confectionery and wine, their hosts giving them the glass vessels they had used, all of fine Venetian workmanship, as leaving presents.[19]

Since sugar was so expensive, the confectionary was one of the few kitchen offices that produced food especially for the King. It was supervised by the sergeant of the confectionary, who received his sugar and spices from the Spicery. With these ingredients he made 'confections, garquinces [quince marmalade], plaatess [sugar plate], sedes [comfits] and all other spycery nedefull; dates, figges, raisonnes, greate and smalle for the Kinge's mouthe, and for his household in Lente seasone; wardens [cooking pears], pearys, apples, quinces, cherryes, and all other fruytes after their seasonne'.[20] These fruits were all supplied at no charge from the King's orchards, in particular the moated Privy Orchard just to the north of the kitchens and the Great Orchard beyond, while 'blaunderelles (white apples), pippins and other fruits were bought in by the sergeant; it was also his responsibility to prepare any fruit given to the King as presents. Some are mentioned in the Privy Purse expenses:[21]

4th April, 1530	servant of Lady Bulstrode for bringing apples
27th June, 1530	keeper of the gardens at York Place, reward for bringing cherries to Hampton Court 4s 8d
10 Aug., 1530	paid to the gardeners of Hampton Court for bringing pears and damsons to the King 7s 6d
16th Aug., 1530	to the gardener of Richmond in reward for bringing filberts and damsons to the King at Hampton Court 4s 8d
14th Oct., 1530	Hobart's servant for bringing oranges and citrons to the King at Hampton Court 4s 8d
21st Dec., 1530	paid to the costermonger as reward for bringing fruits to the King's grace at various times 20s
17th June, 1531	James Hobart, pomegranates, oranges, lemons to Hampton Court 20s

The sergeant was assisted by a yeoman, who made confectionery for the King, the Great Chamber and the Great Hall, and so had to be 'well learned in the makeinge of confections, plates, gardequinces, and others, safely and cleanly to keepe, and honestly to minister it forthe at all tymes of the King's worship, and make trewe answere therof by weyghtes inward and outward'.[22] There was also a groom who helped to make and serve the confections, cleaned the confectionary and undertook general fetching and carrying, as well as a pack-horse man who transported fruit, spices and confectionery as required.

At the end of their meals, after their table had been cleared, or 'voided', the King and Queen would stand up to take sugar-coated spices and a spiced wine called hippocras to warm their stomachs and aid digestion. Even on ordinary days, the spice plates used were of silver, silver gilt or gilded glass, which the sergeant drew from either the Counting House of the Jewel House, filled with spices and passed to the usher of the King's Chamber for service to the King, the groom later collecting the plates and bringing them back to the confectionary. If less important people were to be served, the spice plates were of pewter, drawn from the sergeant of the scullery. For state occasions, the royal spice plates were of the greatest magnificence – here is a description of one listed in Henry VIII's inventory:[23]

> Item one spice plate of greystone the fote and brymme garnysshed with silver gilt standing upon four antique heddes with hornes and a cover of silver and gilt garnyshed with three heddes videlicet [namely] an Agathe a pursleyne [porcelain] and of mother of Emerrauld and garnished with Roses and flower deluces [fleur-de-lis] of counterfete stones . . . with a man in the toppe thereof with a staff and a Sheilde weyieng togethers 68oz [1.9kg].

On important 'days of estate', when the court displayed its grandest ceremonies, the royal spice plates were filled with a pound and a half (700g) of spices – a pound (450g) was normal on ordinary days or for the service of dukes, earls and bishops. The royal confectioners had been making aniseed, coriander, fennel and ginger comfits for centuries, using the 'pannys, basyns, and ladylles that he maketh his confections with dayly'.[24] Most of the smaller, dry spices served at the 'void' were coated in sugar as comfits; pippins eaten with caraway comfits being especially recommended.

To give them their sugar coating the spices were first put into a shallow, round-bottomed brass or latten pan; those used in the late fourteenth century probably had a handle like that of a frying pan but by the mid-sixteenth century this had been replaced by a pair of suspension cords.[25] Having gently heated the pan by holding it a few inches above a chafing dish of glowing charcoal, the caraway seeds or whatever spices were being used would be stirred with the flat of the hand until they were all warm and dry. Next, a little sugar syrup was poured in, using a ladle, and the seeds rubbed around the base of the pan, again with the flat of the hand and the extended fingers, making sure that they stuck neither to the pan nor to each other. The pan would be gently swung, meanwhile, to ensure that it received an even heat. In this way the seeds gained their first layer of sugar. Once this had dried around them, a little more syrup was added, and then the whole process was repeated as many times as necessary until a solid layer of sugar had built up and each seed was the size of a small pea. At this stage, the pan was removed from the heat – or the heat from the pan – and the caraway comfits were stirred with the hand until they had dried out completely to a perfect whiteness. Alternatively, the final coats could have a little vegetable colour stirred into the syrup, to produce red, yellow, green or blue comfits, which were dried off in the same way.

Here is a recipe for those who want to make their own:

COMFITS

10ml (2 tsp) caraway, aniseed, coriander or fennel seeds, or root ginger soaked in water overnight and cut into small cubes, or shelled nuts such as almonds
450g (1lb) cane sugar
275ml (½pt) water

1. *Place the sugar and water in a saucepan and gently heat. Stir with a wooden spatula until the sugar has completely dissolved.*
2. *Stop stirring, bring to the boil, and cook until the sugar reaches 110°C (225°F) on a sugar thermometer. Remove the pan from the heat and dip its base in cold water for a few seconds to stop it cooking any further.*
3. *Place the seeds (or ginger, or nuts) in an omelette pan over a gentle heat, and stir until all are warm and dry.*
4. *Add a teaspoonful of the syrup to the seeds and stir them with the fingers, being very careful not to burn them (or yourself!) by having the pan too hot, until all the seeds are separate and dry.*
5. *Add a little more syrup to the seeds, continuing to stir them with the tips of the fingers until they are dry and separate once more, repeating this operation time after time for a few hours until they have acquired a sugar coating of the required thickness.*
6. *For coloured comfits, slowly stir a little saffron (yellow), cochineal (red) or similar food colouring into the syrup used for the final coats.*
7 *When the comfits are large enough, usually around 3–4mm (⅛in) in the case of seeds, stop adding the syrup and stir them for 5–10 minutes in the pan to dry them off, then put them into sealed containers ready for use.*

10. *Comfit-making* Spices such as caraway, coriander and chopped ginger were given a smooth, hard sugar coating by being repeatedly hand-stirred in a swinging copper pan set over a chafing dish of glowing charcoal. Sugar syrup was added little by little, until it had built up the required thickness around each seed or piece.

Other favourite sweets for the 'void' were 'sugar plate' and one called 'manus Christi' – literally, 'the hand of Christ'. Both were made by boiling the sugar to a much higher degree:[26]

SUGAR PLATE (BOILED)

100g (4oz) cane sugar
150ml (¼pt) water
25–50g (1–2oz) rice flour

1. *Place the rice flour in a small piece of fine muslin, and shake a thin dusting of the flour over a marble slab.*
2. *Place the sugar and water in a small pan over a gentle heat and stir with a wooden spatula until it has dissolved.*
3. *Stop stirring before the sugar boils, then boil until it reaches 170°C (325°F) on a sugar thermometer. Dip the base of the pan into a bowl of cold water for a few moments to prevent it from cooking any further.*
4. *Pour the sugar out on to the marble slab, allowing it to run into thin broad discs. Let it cool until quite brittle, then slide it off and keep in an airtight container until required.*

To make manus Christi, the even more expensive form of sugar plate, the sugar would be boiled exactly as in the recipe above, except that the water was replaced with rosewater. The sugar would be dropped on to the marble slab in small round cakes, then each would be lightly moistened when half cool and coated with gold leaf. Manus Christi was believed to have excellent tonic effects.

Sugar was also used to preserve fruits, very much as it is today. The fruit was lightly cooked in syrup and then sealed with the syrup in ceramic jars. The following recipes are typical:

PRUNES IN SYRUP[27]

225g (8oz) prunes
425ml (¾pt) claret
100g (4oz) sugar

1. *Soak the prunes overnight in the claret.*
2. *Gently cook the prunes, claret and sugar together until the prunes are swollen and tender. Either eat them within the next few days or seal them down in sterilised jars and store in a cool place.*

TO CONSERVE CHERRIES[28]

450g (1lb) sugar
700g (1lb 8oz) cherries
6 cloves
1 small stick cinnamon

1. *Put the sugar and spices into 575ml (1pt) rosewater in a pan and stir with a wooden spatula over a gentle heat until the sugar has dissolved.*
2. *Add the cherries with enough additional water to cover them, bring them to a gentle simmer and continue cooking until they are soft and begin to split.*
3. *To preserve them, pour the hot cherries, spices and syrup into sterilised jars and seal down; for immediate use, allow to cool and serve within the next 2–3 days.*

The peels of oranges and lemons were treated in a similar way to form 'succade', more usually known as sucket in Tudor England. As Andrew Boorde advised, 'Oranges doth make a man to have good appetite, and so do the rinds if they be in succade.'[29]

SUCCADE OF LEMON PEELS[30]

3 lemons (or oranges)
30ml (2 tbs) rosewater
400g (14oz) sugar

1. *Halve the lemons, squeeze out the juice (use for any other purpose – it freezes well) and scrape out the coarser membranes from within the peels.*
2. *Boil the peels in 575ml (1pt) of water for 30 minutes, replacing the water twice to remove the bitterness.*
3. *Add the rosewater and sugar to the lemon peels with ¾ of the water they were cooked in, and simmer gently until they are translucent and the syrup is like thin honey.*
4. *Either preserve them by pouring them into sterilised jars with their syrup and sealing them down, or use within the next 2–3 days.*

Other fruits were preserved in the form of very stiff, sticky pastes which could be served cut up into small slices. These were first brought to England from Portugal, where quinces, *marmelos* in Portuguese, were mixed with sugar and scented substances such as rosewater, musk and ambergris, and then cooked until their natural pectin made the mixture thicken into semi-solid *marmelada*. This was poured into shallow wooden boxes – the most convenient means of packing it for preservation, sale and transport. In 1560, Lord Robert Dudley bought a 'brick of marmelade 2s 4d' for a banquet at Eltham.[31] In England, the Portuguese marmalades were soon being reproduced, using either home-grown quinces or a variety of other fruits such as warden pears, damsons, apricots, peaches, oranges and lemons:[32]

MARMALADE OF LEMONS OR ORANGES

5 large lemons or oranges	150ml (¼pt) water
3 apples, such as Cox's pippins	about 450g (1lb) sugar

1. *Quarter the lemons or oranges and remove the pips and stalk while holding them over a stainless steel pan to catch the juice. Peel, core and quarter the apples.*
2. *Simmer the fruit in the water for about 30 minutes, until tender. Then remove from the heat, and either rub it all through a sieve or blend to form a very smooth paste.*
3. *Weigh the pulp, add its weight in sugar, and stir it all together with a wooden spoon over a gentle heat until very stiff. Then turn out into a lightly greased, shallow tin or flat plate, and allow to cool.*

MARMALADE OF PEACHES OR APRICOTS[33]

450g (1lb) peach or apricot flesh, the stones, peels etc. removed	225g (8oz) sugar 45ml (3 tbs) rosewater

1. *Chop and blend the fruit, or rub through a sieve to make a smooth purée.*
2. *Put the purée, sugar and rosewater into a pan, bring to the boil while stirring with a wooden spoon, then boil rapidly, stirring continuously, until it stiffens and darkens to a dark-orange colour. Drip a few drops from the end of the spoon on to a cold plate to check that it is sufficiently boiled to set very firmly, then pour out on to a lightly greased, shallow tin or flat plate, and allow to cool.*

The simplest way of preparing these marmalades for the 'void' was to cut them up into neat pieces and dust them with sugar – probably ground and sifted and resembling today's caster sugar – then perhaps stamp them with an ornamental mould. If the marmalade was sufficiently stiff it could be sliced into long square-sectioned strips, dusted with sugar and tied into small, neat knots. Alternatively, it could be sliced thinly and cut into oak-leaf shapes; or modelled into miniature half-plums, left to dry overnight round side up, and then stuck together complete with a natural stalk to make very realistic miniature fruits. If the orange or lemon marmalade was used in this way, its colour was greatly improved by adding a smooth dark-red jam to the fruit when it was being cooked.

Another very popular Tudor sweetmeat was made by pounding blanched almonds with rosewater and sugar to form a smooth, stiff off-white paste called marchpane – the early word for our modern 'marzipan'. The basic recipe was as follows:[34]

TO MAKE MARCHPANE

225g (8oz) ground almonds
100g (4oz) icing sugar
45ml (3 tbs) rosewater
4 wafers (p. 141) or rice paper

glaze: 5ml (1 tsp) rosewater
15ml (1 tbs) icing sugar
5ml (1 tsp) rice flour
decoration: coloured comfits (p. 68)
kissing comfits (p. 83)
gold leaf

1. *Mix the almonds and rosewater in a bowl. Stir in the icing sugar and work them together with a pestle or the back of a wooden spoon until they form a smooth, very firm dough. Be careful not to work them too harshly, or the mixture will turn oily.*
2(a). *For an authentic marchpane: the wafers were cut into large squares, their edges moistened and overlapped so as to stick together to form a sheet 20cm (8in) in diameter. The dough was then rolled out inside a 1.3cm (½in) deep hoop of green hazel placed on top of the wafers.*
2(b). *For today: Line the base and bottom inch of a 17.5cm (7in) round loose-bottomed cake tin with the wafers or rice paper, place the dough inside, and smooth level with a spatula.*
3. *Embed patterns of coloured comfits in the top of the marchpane dough.*
4. *Mix the glaze ingredients together, and brush them over the top of the marchpane.*
5. *Place the marchpane on a baking sheet, and bake at 80°C (175°F, low gas) for 30 minutes. Then remove and leave to cool. Repeat this stage, if necessary, until it is quite firm.*
6. *For further decoration, stick some kissing comfits into the marchpane, and/or gild it.*

11. *A Marchpane Mould* This early sixteenth century marchpane mould bears the IHC monogram of Jesus, a popular motif in the decorative arts of this period, and the inscription, cut in reverse, 'An harte that is wyse will obstine from sinnes and increas in the workes of God'.

For gold-leaf decoration, rabbits'-tails were used as 'tips', to lift up the leaf and to pat it down in place. The leaf may be cut into small squares and the place where it is to be set down dampened with a little water, the gold leaf lifted up by one corner, using a small, slightly moistened brush, put in place, and then very gently patted down using a very soft dry brush.

Alternatively, a piece of thin paper was cut out as a stencil, bearing the name of Jesus, a deer, or any other suitable device. The centre of the marchpane was slightly dampened, the stencil laid over it, the gold leaf applied over the exposed areas and patted down. Then the stencil was removed to leave a neat golden motif on top of the marchpane.

This recipe would have produced a typical country-house standard of marchpane, but was very ordinary in comparison with those made for the great royal and other ceremonial feasts. A surviving illustration of an early Tudor marchpane mould shows that they could be large, and often bore decorations such as the crowned IHC (the Greek abbreviation of the name of Jesus), Tudor roses, birds and mottoes.[35] Various contemporary descriptions tell us that they frequently formed a flat base on which were mounted ornate sculptures made of marchpane paste, sugar plate and cast sugar figures. In their most extravagant forms these were served as 'subtleties' – wonderfully impressive sculptural models that would be brought in with great pomp at the start of each course.

Some 'subtleties' were made of wax. The one that preceded the first course at the Sergeant's Feast given to Philip II of Spain and Queen Mary on 16 October 1555 in Inner Temple Hall was 'A Standing Dish of wax, representing the Court of Common Pleas, artificially made, the charge therof £4.' Preceding the second course, there was 'A standing Dish of Wax, to each mess one, £4.'[36] And Anne Boleyn's coronation feast held in Westminster Hall on 1 June 1533 had included 'subtleties and shippes made of waxe, marvylous, gorgeous to behold.[37]

Other subtleties were probably made of sugar, the confectionary making 'A George on Horseback', a suitably magnificent theme to introduce the first course at Henry VIII's Garter dinners.[38] This must have been cast from a set of moulds about a hundred years old – 'a soteltee Seint-Jorge on horseback and sleyng the dragun' had been served at the first course of a royal feast recorded about 1440, the third course continuing the legend with a subtlety of 'a castel that the King and the Qwhene comen in for to see how Seint Jorge flogh [flew?].[39] Some of the other moulds used in the confectionary had probably been inherited from Cardinal Wolsey's kitchens. In 1527 he had served a subtlety of the great medieval St Paul's Cathedral, with its soaring spire; and in 1562 Queen Elizabeth received a similar marchpane bearing a model of St Paul's as a New Year's gift from her surveyor of the works, along with 'a very faire marshpaine made like a tower with men and artillery in it' from her yeoman of the chamber, and a 'faire marchpane being a chessboarde' – another Wolsey speciality – from her master cook.[40]

12. *Subtleties* The main decorative feature of any Tudor feast was a 'subtlety', which could be a model of a building, a saint, a worthy or a virtue, with appropriate mottoes. Here in Hans Springlee's print, *The Battle before the Rouanne*, from *The Triumph of Maximilian* (1526), two subtleties are being carried up to the Emperor. The print provides us with rare evidence of their scale and appearance, and the manner in which they were presented.

The finest account of Tudor confectionery comes from George Cavendish's biography of Cardinal Wolsey, in which he describes the preparation and service of a magnificent feast for the reception of the French ambassadors at Hampton Court in October 1527.[41] It is well worth quoting at length. First, Wolsey

> called for his principal officers of his house, as his steward, Comptroller, and the Clerkes of his kytchen – whome he commaundyd to prepare for them a bankett at Hampton Court, and noither to spare for expences or travell to make them suche tryumphant chere as they may not only wonder at hit here, but also make a gloryous report in their contrie, to the Kynges honour & that of the Realme . . . [Also, they sent for] all the expertest Cookes besydes my lordes that they could gett in all Englond where they myght be gotten to serve to garnysshe this feast. The purveyors brought and sent In suche plenty of Costly provysion as ye wold wonder at the same. The Cookes wrought bothe nyght & day in dyvers subtiltes and many crafty devisis where lakked nother gold, Sylver ne other costly thyng meate for ther purpose . . .
>
> Nowe was all things in a redynes and Supper tyme at hand. My lordes Officers caused the Truppettes to blowe to warne to Supper And the seyd Officers went right discretly in dewe order And conducted thes nobyll personages frome ther Chambers unto the Chamber of presence where they shold Suppe And they beyng there caused them to sytt down ther servyce was brought uppe in suche order & Aboundaunce both Costly & full of subtilties wt suche a pleasaunt noyce of dyvvers Instruments of musyke tht the French men (as it semyd) ware rapte in to an hevenly paradice . . . devysyng and wonderyng uppon the subtilties . . . Anon came uppe the Second Course wt. so many disshes, subtilties, & curious devysis wche. ware above an [hundred] in nomber of so goodly proporcion and Costly that I suppose the Frenchemen never sawe the lyke, the wonder was no lesse than it was worthy in deade. there were Castelles wt. Images in the same, powlles [St Paul's] Chirche & steple in proporcion for the quantitie as well counterfeited as the paynter shold have paynted it uppon a clothe or wall. There were beastes, byrdes, fowles of dvers kyndes And personages most lyvely made & counterfet in dysshes, some fighting (as it ware) wt. swordes, some wt. Gonnes and Crosebowes, Some vaughtyng & leapyng, Some dauncyng wt. ladyes, Some in complett harnes lustyng [fighting] wt. speres, And wt. many more devysis than I am able wt. my wytt to discribbe. Among all oon I noted there was a Chesse bord subtilly made of spiced plate wt. men to the same, And for the good proporcyon bycause that frenche men be very experte at that play my lord gave the same to a gentilman of fraunce commaundyng that a Case shold be made for the same in all hast to preserve it from perysshyng in the conveyaunce therof to hys Contrie.

To make figures of this kind a variety of techniques were used. Since sugar shrinks at different rates, depending on its own moisture content and on

PB.

that of the atmosphere – drying rock-hard on the surface while remaining soft inside, and cracking if it is built up layer on layer – it is not particularly suitable for freehand modelling and so, like clay, it had to be cast in moulds.

Sir Hugh Plat, in his *Delightes for Ladies* (1602), notes that some moulds were made by taking sectional plaster of Paris impressions from fruits, nuts, birds and so on, in such a way that they could be reassembled and tied together with tapes so as to enclose the complete negative shape of whatever was being copied.[42] Alternatively, sectional moulds could be taken in pottery clay from any carved or modelled figure, and then be fired to convert them into hard-wearing terracotta. One late fifteenth to early sixteenth century mould of this type, dug up at the Old Bailey in London, was used to reproduce sugar effigies (five and a half inches (14cm) high) of St Catherine, depicted holding up her personal symbol of a small wheel. Other moulds were carved out of porous stone or even wood.

This is how the moulds were used. Either the insides were coated in almond oil[43] or, preferably, they were soaked in water, perhaps for up to a day for plaster ones but only three or four hours for those of wood. The parts were then drained, dried with a cloth, assembled and tied together, then filled with sugar boiled as for sugar plate (p. 70). If the mould had an opening – like the open base of the St Catherine – the surplus molten sugar could be tipped out after a short time, and the mould then turned round and round and end over end to stop the thick hot syrup from settling unevenly before it set hard. When it was completely hard and cold, after an hour or so, the mould was opened and the hollow sugar cast removed. For completely enclosed moulds, one section was removed, the remaining cavity half-filled with the molten sugar, and the first section replaced. Then the confectioner would rapidly turn the whole mould over and over in every direction so as to evenly coat the inner surface. The main problem with this method was that, as the hot air inside began to cool, it sucked in part of the sugar shell and deformed it, unless a hot needle was inserted at a joint to break the vacuum. As medieval English recipe books prove, the introduction of plaster of Paris moulds, coated internally with a thick liquid – in this case, sugar – to produce thin-walled hollow con-

13. *The Waddesdon Court Figures* The sugar figures made in the Confectionary probably bore a close resemblance to these early sixteenth century oak figures which originally stood around the frieze of the dining room at Waddesdon Court, Stoke Gabriel, in Devon. This selection shows (top) the Christian Worthies — King Arthur, Charlemagne and Godfrey de Bouillon — and (bottom) the Pagan Worthies — Hector of Troy, Julius Caesar and Alexander the Great, as described in the introduction to Caxton's *Morte de'Arthur* of 1485. They may now be seen in the Torquay Museum.

14. *St Catherine* This figure, shown holding her symbolic wheel in her left hand, was made by pouring boiling sugar into the accompanying mould, which beforehand had been either soaked in water or brushed with oil to enable the complete cast to be easily removed. The mould, now in the Museum of London, was found in the Old Bailey.

fections, was already a well established culinary practice here in the late fourteenth century. It took the brightest Staffordshire potters over three hundred years to work out that they could make fine pottery in the same way, but even after this long delay, they had no hesitation in claiming slip-casting as a completely new discovery, entirely of their own invention!

When it came to more complicated figures, such as those for the French embassy described by George Cavendish, the boiled sugar plate was troublesome both to cast and to assemble, and because it was semi-translucent it was difficult to decorate with anything other than gold or silver leaf. A new kind of sugar plate was therefore introduced, one that was easier to handle and dried to a pure matt-white finish ideal for receiving decoration. The first recipe for this sugar plate to be published in England was in Girolamo Ruscelli's *The Secretes of the Reverend Maister Alexis of Piedmont* of 1562, but by this time it had probably been in use in the royal confectionary for many years. Instead of having to be boiled, the sugar was simply ground to a fine powder and then sifted to produce the equivalent of today's icing sugar. Once mixed with a natural vegetable substance, gum tragacanth, as a binder, and lemon juice and rosewater for flavour, it was transformed into one of the most versatile of all confectionery media.[44]

Hampton Court Palace
Here the imposing west front of Cardinal Wolsey's palace appears between the extending wings built by Henry VIII. That to the right was the Great House of Ease — the toilet block — while that to the left is the Back Gate, the entrance to the kitchens and the office of the Board of the Greencloth which controlled the entire royal household.

The Cooks
Henry VIII's Master Cooks were given a clothing allowance to ensure that all their staff were clean and well-dressed at all times. Here is a group of the cooks who have been operating the palace's Tudor kitchens every Christmas and New Year since 1991.

Greencloth Yard
Standing here beneath the Back Gate, the Porter could watch the various doorways leading into the kitchen offices, as could the Clerk of the Kitchen from his office over the inner gateway. Greencloth Yard in the foreground housed the coal cellar, the chandlery and the spicery, while the pastry, confectionary and dry fish store were in Pastry Yard beyond.

Confectionery
The confectioners made a great variety of sugarwork for the King and leading courtiers. The most useful of all their mixtures was sugar plate, a combination of sugar, rosewater, lemon juice and natural gum. It could be readily shaped in wooden moulds, and then receive bright decoration with vegetable colouring and gold leaf.

Baking
Although the Tudor bakehouse was demolished in the late nineteenth century, this later oven gives a good impression of how it operated. Having been heated within by burning faggots of brushwood, the ashes were raked out, the loaves inserted, and a sheet-iron door sealed in place with mud. Once the bread had been baked, the door was removed, and the loaves taken out using a long-handled oven-peel.

St Paul's Cathedral
Confectioners at Hampton Court were making sugar-sculptures of the great medieval St Paul's Cathedral in 1527, their successors later making them as New Year presents for Queen Elizabeth.

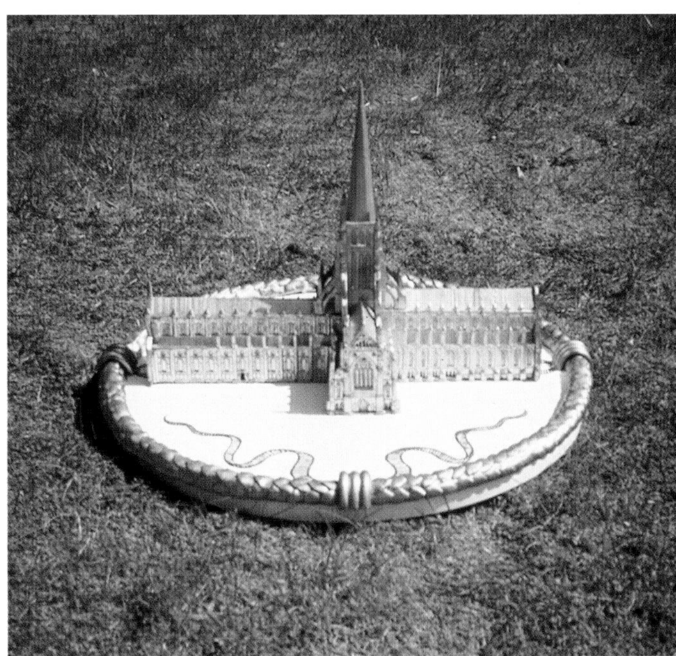

Moulded Marchpane
A drawing of an early sixteenth-century marchpane mould published in 1827 provides the only visual evidence of the appearance of these enormous confections. Here the mould has been re-carved and used to make a white gingerbread marchpane, its IHC name of Jesus and other details being decorated with natural colours and gilding.

Sugar Figures
These figures combine written evidence from descriptions of a Hampton Court banquet, and visual evidence from diverse sources such as Henry VIII's writing desk, stained glass, designs on charters, and carvings executed for Henry's Knight Marshal, to re-create an impression of their original appearance.

A Wild Boar
By the early sixteenth century wild boar were already facing extinction in England. They were prized both as the fiercest of all native game, and as the source of the finely-flavoured brawns and boar's heads served at Christmastime.

Charcoal Stoves
For all the finer aspects of cookery, the cooks used charcoal stoves — strong masonry benches with circular firebaskets set into their tops. Having a good draught from below, they gave a clear, steady heat with no smoke — only a perfectly invisible blast of scorching carbon monoxide which stifled anyone who accidentally inhaled it.

The Hall-Place Kitchen
Built for Henry VIII around 1530, this kitchen rose forty feet to the ridge of the roof, this great height being required to dissipate the heat and steam from the fires and cooking pots.

Roast Sucking Pig
As the pig is turned on its spit, the juices are caught in the dripping pan beneath, along with the butter used for basting. As the thin meat over the ribs is already hot, it will now be shielded from the heat by an iron pig-plate which leaves the shoulders and hams exposed so that they can cook through evenly.

Farced Chicken and a Train Roast
Using methods introduced from the Middle East during the Crusades, the chickens have been stuffed between their skins and flesh with a rich fat pork, herb and egg forcemeat. This bastes them and retains all their own juices and flavour as they roast. The lower spit has been wound with a 'necklace' of dried fruits and almonds which will start to caramelise before the fire, before being basted in a rich batter to form a flavoursome sweet.

Peacock Royal
Having had its skin and head removed in one piece, and dusted internally with cumin, the peacock has been trussed on a spit, just as if it was sitting on a perch, and roasted before the fire. Just before serving, the bird has been dished on a large platter, and the skin re-applied, to make the most delicious and impressive of all roasts.

Setting the Table
During demonstrations, the kitchen table is set at 3 p.m. in the authentic manner of the 1540s, with a trencher and cup of turned ash, a linen napkin, a manchet loaf, and a pewter spoon at each plate. At this time there are usually over three hundred visitors in the kitchen to hear the talks given by the cooks, and then to watch supper being served and eaten using appropriate table manners.

Supper
At the end of a midwinter afternoon, after a day's cooking had been completed and supper sent up to the Great Hall and Great Watching Chamber, the kitchen staff would sit down to take their own supper, before tackling the mountains of washing up and cleaning of their utensils ready to start again in twelve hours' time.

Garnished Brawn
Brawn, made by rolling and spicing large joints of wild boar or pork, was one of the most prestigious of all Christmas dishes, and was therefore lavishly garnished to make an impressive appearance as it was carried up from the kitchens. Robert May, a cook trained in the late Tudor tradition, described how it should be sliced and decorated with carved fruit, grapes, jelly, bayleaves, spots of gold and silver foil, and a large sprig of yew, sprinkled with flour to represent the season's frost and snow.

A Boiled Leg of Mutton
Having been partly roast, pressed, and simmered in stock, wine and wine vinegar, this leg of lamb was dished on a bed of cubed bread, and garnished with lemon slices and a broad border of large sugar crystals. It now waits to be carved and served accompanied with salt and mustard. This may have been one of the dishes taught to the great Elizabethan ladies by the Clerk of the Kitchen.

SUGAR PLATE (PASTE)

2.5ml ($\frac{1}{2}$ tsp) gum tragacanth
5ml (1 tsp) strained lemon juice
10ml (2 tsp) rosewater
half a sterilised egg white
350–450g (12–16oz) icing sugar

1. *Stir the gum tragacanth into the lemon juice and rosewater in a small basin. Leave overnight, or place in a pan of hot water until the gum tragacanth has dissolved, and leave it to cool.*
2. *Stir in the lightly beaten egg white (and any required food colouring), then work in the sifted icing sugar, little by little, until it forms a dough. Turn this out on to a board with more icing sugar, and knead until completely smooth.*
3. *Roll it into a ball, and closely wrap in a plastic food bag immediately, since the surface dries out to brittleness after only a short exposure to the air.*

The moulds used for the boiled sugar plate could now be used for this new cold sugar plate, but instead of having to be pre-soaked and the parts tied together, they were used bone-dry – just dusted with a little finely powdered sugar, starch or spice to prevent the sugar plate from sticking inside them. To make a round fruit such as an orange, for example, pieces of the soft, pastry-like mixture could be pressed into each section of the mould, the edges trimmed level with a knife and brushed with a little gum tragacanth solution to make the parts stick together; then the mould would be reassembled and after a while the completely spherical fruit turned out into a box of freshly sifted flour, which would hold it in shape until it had hardened. The new sugar plate could also be cast in shallow wooden moulds, perhaps only an eighth of an inch (3–4mm) in depth; the surplus would be cut off with a knife, and then the sugar plate would be turned out by holding the mould upside down above a worktop, at a slight angle from the horizontal, then sharply banging down the lower end to make the sugar plate drop out face upwards. The moulding could then be carefully draped over a 'former', where it would set into the shape of part of a limb, a torse, a shield – or whatever was being made. Once perfectly dry, the edges of each piece would be neatly trimmed and stuck to other pieces using a strong gum-tragacanth and icing-sugar 'cement', in much the same way as you might assemble the parts of a injection-moulded plastic construction kit.

The completed figure could now be decorated – its smooth, white and slightly absorbent surface being ideal for receiving the painted brushwork. The confectionery colours used at this period were usually of vegetable origin:[45]

Red	saunders (red sandalwood), the East Indian tree *Pterocarpus santalinus*
	brazilwood, the East Indian tree *Caesalpinia sappan*
	red rose petals
Yellow	saffron, the dried stigmas of *Crocus sativus*, grown around Saffron Walden
	cowslip or marigold petals
Green	the juice of spinach, *Spinacia oleracea*, or of green wheat
Blue	'bluebottles', the petals of the common cornflower, *Centaurea cyanus*
Violet	violet petals, *Viola odorata*
	turnsole, the Mediterranean plant *Chrozophora tinctoria*, whose dark-green juice turns purple on exposure to the air. It was usually prepared at source: pieces of cloth would be dipped into it, then dried ready for export.

The hardwoods, saunders and brazil, were reduced to fine chippings or to powder and boiled in a little water together with gum arabic, while the flower petals were ground in rosewater and the coloured juice squeezed out through a piece of cloth. Turnsole rags had only to be scalded in water to induce them to give up their colour.[46]

All these colours were relatively safe to consume, especially since they were used in such small quantities, but other materials were positively poisonous, as may be seen from these examples mentioned by John Partridge in his book *The Widowes Treasure*, published in 1585:[47]

'A very good green'	the juice of rue, verdigris (basic copper acetate) and saffron
Emerald green	verdigris, litharge (lead monoxide) and mercury, beaten together and ground 'with the pisse of a young childe'
Gold	orpiment (arsenic trisulphate), ground with clear quartz, saffron powder and the gall of a hare or a pike, stored in a phial in a dunghill for five days, and kept for use

It is amazing to find such recipes in any cookery book, since anyone who consumed even the smallest amount of these substances would certainly become dangerously ill, if not die.

Either gum-water (a solution of gum tragacanth) or egg white was used to provide a thickening and drying medium, which made the colours easy to apply with a brush and gave a hard finish, usually with a slight gloss. (Today you should use only the safe vegetable colours, needless to say, and

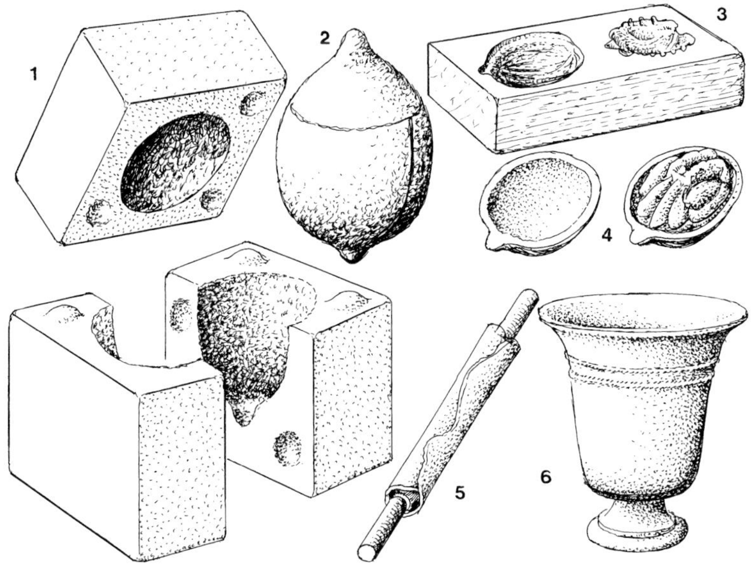

15. *Sugar moulds* Tudor sugar-moulding was a highly skilled craft. Here are (1) the sectional plaster moulds used to cast lemons (2) in boiling sugar; the carved wooden press-mould (3) for making walnut shells and kernels (4); and the equally realistic cinnamon sticks (5) and porcelain-like drinking cups (6), also made in finely flavoured sugar plate.

the whites of sterilised eggs.) For denser colours and richer flavourings, the sugar plate could be mixed with finely ground and sifted spices, or the petals of marigolds, cowslips, primroses or roses first ground into some icing sugar with a little rosewater before being made up into a paste with more sugar and a little gum tragacanth.[48] Among the most popular confections served at the void and other occasions were these, all based on the sugar plate recipe on page 81.

MUSCADINES, OR KISSING COMFITS[49]

1. Divide a piece of sugar plate into three portions, colouring one red, another blue, and leaving the third one white.
2. Roll out each piece of plate in turn on a smooth surface, dusting it with a little cornflour to prevent it from sticking, then cut it into small diamonds, if possible using a pastry jigger with a notched wheel. Place the shapes on a sheet of paper dusted with cornflour, and leave them to dry completely.

They would then either have been eaten in this form, or used to decorate marchpanes, for instance.

CARDS[50]

1. Roll out a piece of white sugar plate on a smooth surface, dusting it with a little cornflour to prevent sticking. Then cut it out in the form of small playing cards, and set them aside to dry completely.
2. Using the vegetable colours described above, paint each card with its suit, etc., to make a miniature pack of cards.

CINNAMON STICKS[51]

1. Make a small batch of sugar plate, but incorporate 5ml (1 tsp) each of finely ground cinnamon and ginger to each 50g (2oz) of icing sugar so as to colour it a light brown.
2. Take small lumps of this brown sugar plate, roll them out very thinly on a smooth surface, dusting it with more ground cinnamon to prevent sticking, and leave the edges in their untrimmed state.
3. Roll each piece of plate around a pencil (originally a 'stick made of peeces of arrowes') and leave it there until half dry. Then pull out the pencil and leave it to dry out to form a very realistic but completely edible cinnamon stick.

TO MAKE ARTIFICIAL WALNUTS[52]

For these, moulds of plaster or carved wood would be prepared, from which to make accurate imitations of half-walnut shells and half-kernels.

1. Prepare a small batch of white sugar plate and one of brown, as described in the previous recipe.
2. Dust the inside of the walnut-shell mould with finely ground cinnamon. Work a little of the brown paste into a thin walnut-shell shape, dust its outside with ground cinnamon, then press it into the mould. Trim off the surplus with a small knife, always cutting from the centre towards the edge of the mould. Then knock the hollow sugar shell out on to the board and set it aside until fully hardened.
3. Dust the kernel mould with a little cornflour, press a small piece of the white sugar plate into it, then trim off the surplus with the knife. Knock it out on to the board, and leave to dry.
4. Mix together a little gum tragacanth and warm water, and use it to assemble the kernels in pairs, place these within one half shell, gum the edges, and place another shell on top, to produce a complete walnut, Small biscuits, caraway comfits or a 'pritty poesie' may be sealed inside the walnut shells instead of the kernel.

In his recipe of 1562, Alexis of Piedmont had described sugar plate 'whereof a man may make all manner of fruits and other fine things with their form, as platters, glasses, cups and suchlike things, wherewith you may furnish a table, and when you have done, eat them up, A pleasant thing for them that sit at table'.[53] A table completely set with sugar-plate tableware must have been very impressive, its pure white closely resembling expensive oriental porcelain or the milk-white variety of Venetian glass. It is most probable that for producing cups and other vessels in this way the confectioners made special moulds, but flat sweetmeat trenchers, about five inches (13cm) in diameter, could be easily rolled out and cut to size, leaving a blank area that would be ideal for elaborate painting and gilding. Small platters were easily executed too, simply by dusting a sheet of rolled-out sugar plate with icing sugar, patting it dusted-side-down on top of a metal or pottery plate, then trimming the edges and leaving it to dry.

A further use of sugar plate was to give a thin coating to marchpanes, in order to improve the smoothness and brilliance of their surface and provide a delicious blend of flavours and textures. Large marchpanes shaped in moulds benefited by this method, in that the carved detail impossible to reproduce on marchpane could be achieved with perfect accuracy on the sugar surface. The same combination was used to make individual sweetmeats such as:[54]

WHITE GINGERBREAD

225g (8oz) marchpane (almond paste), p. 73
15ml (1 tbs) ground ginger
225g (8oz) sugar plate (p. 81)

1. *Knead the ginger into the marchpane and roll it out on a board dusted with icing sugar to about 7mm (¼in) in thickness.*
2. *Divide the sugar plate into two, and roll out one piece into the same size as the marchpane. Dampen one side of the marchpane, and place it damp side down on the sugar plate. Next, roll out the other piece of sugar plate, dampen the other side of the marchpane, place the sugar plate on top and smooth it down. Then roll the marchpane and sugar plate (white gingerbread) sandwich to around 7mm (¼in) in thickness.*
3. *Cut the gingerbread into small diamonds with a pastry jigger. Or cut it into sections, dust with a little cornflour, and press the sections into moulds, trimming off the surplus with a knife, and leave to dry.*

Any unused trimmings may be kneaded together until smooth, then rolled out and cut into diamond shapes as gingerbreads.

At this period gingerbreads were small, sweet-like confections rather than the ginger-flavoured cakes that bear this name today. Some were made of boiled honey and ground ginger, while others were composed of sugar, spices and grated white breadcrumbs. Here is a recipe found in Sir Hugh Plat's *Delightes for Ladies*:[55]

GINGERBREAD USED AT THE COURT

225g (8oz) fresh white breadcrumbs
5ml (1 tsp) ground ginger
5ml (1 tsp) ground cinnamon
5ml (1 tsp) aniseed
5ml (1 tsp) ground liquorice
25g (1oz) sugar
150ml (¼pt) claret

1. Dry the breadcrumbs under the grill or in the oven, without browning. Mix them with the remaining ingredients in a saucepan, and work with a wooden spatula over a gentle heat until they become a very stiff red dough. (This is a long and laborious process – hard stirring is required to prevent the mixture from sticking and burning.)
2. Turn the mixture out on to a board dusted with ground ginger and cinnamon, knead until perfectly smooth, then roll out to about 7 mm (¼in) in thickness. Either cut into small squares, or press into moulds and turn out, then leave to dry on a wire rack.

Back in the Pastry Yard after our visit to the confectionary, we find that the next doorway led into the room below, the pastry, where almost every variety of pasty, pie and tart was baked for the royal household. Its sergeants, John Jenyns in 1540–2, succeeded by John Heath before he transferred to the bakehouse, and its clerk Anthony Weldon, were responsible for ensuring that 'all their baked Meates [were] well seasoned and served . . . without imbesselment or giveing away any of the same; and also that there be no wastefull expences made of any Flower or Sawce within the said Office'.[56] Before eight every morning, the clerk had to deliver to the clerk of the kitchen the brief that detailed the previous day's consumption of foodstuffs in the bakehouse, and once a month submit his 'parcel' of requests for fresh supplies to the counting house. The Pastry's administrative office was on the first floor, beyond the confectionary, while the sergeant's and clerk's lodgings, along with those of their six yeomen, their grooms and four 'conducts', or labourers, were in the first-floor chambers and second-floor garrets – warm and dry over the main pastry workhouses.

There were three working rooms in the pastry, the first and smallest (no. 25) of which was probably the storehouse and boulting house for the various flours used there. These probably included wholemeal for the coarsest pastry, and from which the conducts would sift the bran to produce wheatmeal flour for common pastry, or sift again through finer sieves to produce unbleached white flour for the finer pastries. Next door (no. 24), was the main pastry workhouse, where the practical pastry-making was carried out.

Of all the foods prepared here, by far the largest and most impressive were the venison pasties made with deer either hunted in the royal parks or presented as gifts to the King – such as the stags brought from Waltham Forest to Hampton Court in August 1530, or the Windsor venison that arrived in June 1531.[57] Some recipes first boiled a whole side of venison before enclosing it in a massive pastry crust:[58]

TO BAKE RED DEER

Imprimis: parboil the Red Deer with wine and vinegar and also water; when it is cold, larde it, then lay it in the same liquor wherein it was parboiled and salt and so close it; then set it in the oven, the while it is abaking, make a syrup with a little of the leanest of your mutton broth, adding wine, sugar, cinnamon, ginger, cloves and mace; and also nutmegs and vinegar. Boil all these things together in a little pot, and when your paste is hard, put the syrup into the pastie, and so let it stand till you see how to draw it. This venison is better cold than hot.

Alternatively, the venison could be minced, larded and spiced before being baked – here is a less unwieldy dish than the last one!:[59]

TO BAKE VENISON

1350g (3lb) lean venison, finely chopped or minced
6 slices fat bacon
60 ml (4 tbs) wine vinegar
1.5ml ($\frac{1}{4}$ tsp) ground cloves
5ml (1 tsp) ground fennel seed
10ml (2 tsp) salt
2.5ml ($\frac{1}{2}$ tsp) ground black pepper
pastry: 700g (1lb 8oz) wholemeal flour
425ml ($\frac{3}{4}$pt) water

1. *Cut the bacon into long 7mm ($\frac{1}{4}$in) wide strips and soak them in the vinegar.*
2. *Mix the venison with the cloves, fennel, salt and pepper.*
3. *Mix the water into the flour to form the pastry, and roll it out into a large rectangle.*
4. *Lay a quarter of the bacon across one half of the pastry, press a*

16. *Venison* Venison for the King's table came from his frequent hunting expeditions, from the royal parks, or as gifts from courtiers. These harts are from George Turberville's *Boke of Hunting* of 1576.

third of the venison into a rectangular slab on top of the bacon, then add alternate layers of venison and bacon.

5. Moisten the pastry around the edge of the venison, fold the vacant half of the pastry over the top, and seal it down and decorate the edges (see p. 92, drawing no. 1).

6. Bake at 200°C (400°F, gas mark 6) for 20 minutes, then reduce to 180°C (350°F, gas mark 4) for a further 1 hour 45 minutes, until cooked. Serve either hot or cold.

In this recipe wholemeal pastry is merely a convenient container for the meat, serving the same purpose as the pottery baking dishes introduced a century or more later, and not really intended to be eaten. In most other Tudor recipes, however, great care was taken to given the pastries subtle flavours, both savoury and sweet, so that they could form an appropriate accompaniment to their contents:[60]

TO MAKE BEEF PIES

550g (1lb 4oz) lean stewing or
braising steak
2.5ml (½ tsp) salt
1.5 ml (¼ tsp) pepper
large pinch saffron
50g (2oz) suet
15ml (1 tbs) wine vinegar
25g (1oz) chopped dates
25g (1oz) chopped prunes
50g (2oz) raisins
Paste Royal: 100g (4oz) butter
150ml (¼ pt) beef stock
450g (1lb) plain flour
1 egg, separated

1. *Mince the beef and mix together with the salt, pepper, saffron, suet, vinegar and dried fruit.*
2. *Put the flour into a bowl and make a well in the centre.*
3. *Melt the butter in the stock, heat to boiling, pour into the flour and stir it in robustly and rapidly, adding the egg yolk to form a hot dough, and knead until smooth.*
4. *For a hand-raised pie, cut off a quarter of the dough, shape the larger piece into a ball, make a deep hollow down the middle with the thumbs, and form into a pie case about 15cm (6in) in diameter and 7.5cm (3in) high, using a pie block or jam jar to assist in the shaping. Place two or three layers of greaseproof paper around the pie, secure it with string, and fill with the beef mixture.*
5. *For a tin-baked pie, use three-quarters of the pastry to line a 15cm (6in) loose-bottomed cake tin, and fill it with the beef mixture.*
6. *Roll out the remaining pastry to form a lid, moisten the edges with a little of the beaten egg white, and lay the lid in place. Now seal it to the inner top edges of the pie case, trim evenly, and squeeze between the fingers to form a fluted edge.*
6. *Cut a small hole in the centre of the lid, and surround it with a ring of pastry made from the trimmings.*
7. *Bake at 220°C (425°F, gas mark 7) for 15 minutes, then reduce the temperature to 180°C (350°F, gas mark 4) for a further 2 hours.*

CHICKEN PIE WITH FINE PASTRY[61]

900g (2lb) lean chicken meat
50g (2oz) butter
20ml (4 tsp) sugar
2.5ml (½ tsp) ground mace
2.5ml (½ tsp) ground cinnamon
2.5ml (½ tsp) salt
50g (2oz) chopped prunes
50g (2oz) raisins
50g (2oz) chopped dried figs
25g (1oz) currants
pastry: 450g (1lb) plain flour
2.5ml (½ tsp) salt
45ml (3 tbs) sugar
100g (4oz) butter
pinch ground saffron
175ml (6 fl oz) ale
1 egg, lightly beaten

1. First make the pastry. Place the sugar, salt, butter, saffron and ale in a saucepan, bring them to the boil, stirring to melt the butter.
2. Put the flour into a bowl, make a well in the centre, pour in the hot liquid, and quickly beat it in with a wooden spoon, while pouring in the egg, to form a dough.
3. Knead the dough, cut off a quarter, and use the remainder to make either a 17.5cm (7in) pie case, or to line a loose-bottomed cake tin of the same size (see point 5 in the previous recipe).
4. Now cut the chicken meat into large pieces, mix with the remaining ingredients and the butter cut in small pieces, and pack into the pie case.
5. Roll out the remaining pastry to form the lid, moisten the edges, and seal in place. Now trim the edges and cut a small hole in the centre of the lid and surround it with a ring of pastry made from the trimmings.
6. Bake at 200°C (400°F, gas mark 6) for 30 minutes, then reduce the temperature to 180°C (350°F, gas mark 4) for a further 1 hour 30 minutes.

For fish days, the Pastry would make pies and pasties such as this one:[62]

TO BAKE STOCKFISH

450g (1lb) skinned cod fillets or salt fish soaked for 24 hours
1 small onion, chopped
15ml (1 tbs) chopped parsley
pepper and salt to taste
25g (1oz) butter
15ml (1 tbs) cider vinegar or wine vinegar
a little milk
pastry: 350g (12oz) plain flour
125g (5oz) lard
60–90ml (4–6 tbs) cold water

1. Mix together the onion, parsley, salt and pepper.
2. Rub the lard into the flour, mix in just enough water to make a stiff shortcrust pastry, and knead lightly.
3. Roll the pastry out to form a large rectangle.
4. Put a layer of the onion mixture across one half of the pastry, and arrange some of the fish on top. Add the remaining onion mixture and fish in alternate layers, dotting them with butter, to form a shallow rectangular mound.
5. Moisten the edges of the pastry with a little milk, fold the empty half of the pastry over the fish mixture, and seal and roll the edges all round. Then pierce a hole in the top and pour in the vinegar.
6. Glaze the pastry with milk, and bake at 220°C (400°F, gas mark 6) for 45 minutes.

There were numerous fruit pies too – some of the best were raised pies with excellent saffron-flavoured pastry:[63]

TO MAKE PIES OF GREEN APPLES

700g (1lb 8oz) Bramley or similar apples
30ml (2 tbs) sugar
1.5ml (¼ tsp) ground ginger
2.5ml (½ tsp) ground cinnamon
25g (1oz) butter

pastry: 100g (4oz) butter
large pinch saffron
150ml (¼pt) water
450g (1lb) plain flour
1 egg, lightly beaten

1. *First make the pastry. Simmer the saffron in the water for 5 minutes to bring out the flavour and colour, then add the 100g (4oz) butter, and leave it to melt.*
2. *Put the flour into a bowl, make a well in the centre, and pour in the hot liquid. Work it in very rapidly with a wooden spoon, beat in the egg, and then knead to form a dough.*
3. *Cut off a quarter of the dough, roll the remainder into a ball, and either form it into a raised pie case* *(see p. 89, point 4)* *or use it to line a deep 15–17.5cm (6–7in) loose-bottomed cake tin.*
4. *Peel and slice the apples. Mix together the sugar, ginger and cinnamon, and pack the apples into the pie case as closely as possible, sprinkling with the spiced sugar until it is full.*
5. *Lay the 25g (1oz) of butter in pieces on top of the apples. Roll out the remaining pastry to form a lid, wet the edges, place it over the pie, seal down and trim the edges. Cut a small hole in the centre, and edge the pie with a border made from the pastry trimmings.*
6. *Bake at 220°C (425°F, gas mark 7) for 15 minutes, then reduce the temperature to 180°C (350°F, gas mark 4) for a further hour or a little more, when the apples are tender when tested with a skewer passed down the hole. Best served cold.*

In March 1530 a servant of Lady Sydney was given a reward of 6s 8d for bringing an orange pie for the King. At this time of year it would probably have been made from preserved oranges, as here:[64]

FOR A TARTE OF APPLES AND ORANGE PEELS

1. *Make the pie exactly as in the previous recipe, but replace 225g (8oz) of the apples with orange peels, and prepare them with 150g (5oz) of honey as follows:*

17. *Pasties and Pies* Tudor pasties and pies were made in a variety of shapes. Here we see venison pasties (1) marked with an appropriate V, based on an illustration from Robert May's *The Accomplish't Cook* (1660); and a smaller triangular pasty (2) as recommended by Thomas Dawson. Some raised pies, like May's salmon pie (3), used their shape to indicate their contents, while others resembled modern pork pies (4) or had their lids blown up using a straw before being put into the oven (5). This one, together with the open-topped tart (6), is based on an engraving showing James I entertaining the Spanish ambassadors in 1623.

2. *If the pith is very thick, cut away the surplus, then soak the peels in water for 36 hours.*
3. *Gently simmer the peels with the honey and enough water to cover them for about 30 minutes until tender, then leave them in the syrup for a further 36 hours.*
4. *Chop the peels into small pieces, and put them in the pie case in layers with the apples. Continue as from point 5 in the recipe above.*

Open tarts were equally popular. Usually a number of empty tart cases would be baked, filled with a variety of prepared mixtures which had only to be cooked for a relatively short period. This was a sensible system for the large-scale catering necessary for great households such as Hampton Court, since the cases could be baked in the ovens while they were still hot from preparing supper for four o'clock, then stored until required for uses. In addition, this method ensured that their bases were cooked properly, neither soggy nor underdone as they would have been if baked when full of moist fillings.[65]

SHORT PASTE FOR TARTS

175g (6oz) flour
100g (4oz) butter
pinch of saffron
1 egg yolk

1. *Grind the saffron to a powder, mix with the flour, then rub in the butter.*
2. *Work in the egg yolk with a fork, knead lightly, roll out on a floured board, and use the pastry to line a 20cm (8in) flan ring.*
3. *Line the inside of the pastry with greaseproof paper and fill it with baking beans, then bake at 200°C (400°F, gas mark 6) for 10–15 minutes, until set. Then remove the beans and paper and return the pastry to the oven for 5 minutes to firm the base. Remove from the oven and leave to cool on a rack.*

The cases may then be filled with various contents – try any of the following tarts:

A TART OF GOOSEBERRIES[66]

350g (12oz) gooseberries or damsons
275ml (½pt) white wine, or claret for the damsons
25g (1oz) butter
75g (3oz) fresh white breadcrumbs
45ml (3 tbs) sugar
3 egg yolks, lightly beaten

1. *Simmer the gooseberries in the wine, or the damsons in the claret, until tender, then add the breadcrumbs, stirring continuously to form a soft mixture.*
2. *Using the back of a wooden spoon, rub the mixture through a sieve into a bowl, then beat in the butter, sugar, and finally the eggs.*
3. *Pour the mixture into the prepared tart case and bake at 180°C (350°F, gas mark 4) for 45 minutes until set. Serve cold.*

A TART OF APPLES[67]

900g (2lb) apples
150ml (¼pt) white wine
45ml (3 tbs) sugar
1.5ml (¼ tsp) ground cinnamon

1. *Peel, core and chop the apples, put them in a pan with the wine, and cook until soft and fairly thick.*
2. *Remove from the heat, rub through a sieve with the back of a wooden spoon, and mix in the sugar and cinnamon.*
3. *Pour the mixture into the prepared tart case and bake at 180°C (350°F, gas mark 4) for 30 minutes.*

A TART OF STRAWBERRIES[68]

450g (1lb) strawberries
3 egg yolks, lightly beaten
50g (2oz) fresh white breadcrumbs
45ml (3 tbs) sugar
25g (1oz) butter

1. *Rub the strawberries through a sieve, using the back of a wooden spoon.*
2. *Warm the butter, without melting it, beat in the breadcrumbs and sugar, and then beat in the egg yolks and strawberry purée.*
3. *Pour the mixture into the prepared tart case and bake at 180°C (350°F, gas mark 4) for 40 minutes until set. Serve cold.*

A TART OF SPINACH[69]

225g (8oz) fresh spinach, or a 400g (14oz) tin of spinach, drained
3 eggs, lightly beaten
50g (2oz) butter
2.5ml (½ tsp) ground cinnamon
2.5ml (½ tsp) ground ginger
15ml (1 tbs) sugar

1. *Wash the fresh spinach, shake off the surplus water, and cook in a covered pan for 10–15 minutes until tender.*
2. *Rub the cooked (or tinned) spinach through a sieve, or blend until smooth. Mix in the warmed but unmelted butter, sugar, spices and eggs, and pour into the prepared tart case.*
3. *Bake at 180°C (350°F, gas mark 4) for 45 minutes until set. Serve cold.*

A TART OF CHEESE[70]

200g (7oz) Cheshire or similar cheese	3 egg yolks, lightly beaten
275ml (½pt) full-cream milk	10ml (2 tsp) sugar
	25g (1oz) butter

1. *Finely grate the cheese, and soak it in the milk for 3 hours. Then blend them together and rub through a sieve.*
2. *Mix in the sugar, egg yolks and warmed but unmelted butter. Pour the mixture into the prepared tart case and bake at 180°C (350°F, gas mark 4) for 40 minutes until set. Serve cold.*

All the pies and pasties made in the pastry were baked in the adjacent pastry bakehouse (no. 23). Four ovens were built in its west wall by Gabryell Dalton in 1530; all were constructed with shallow domed roofs made of tiles set edge to edge to resist the effects of the constant fierce heat followed by gradual cooling.[71] The largest measured over twelve feet (3.7m) in diameter – ideal for all the largest pasties. In front of the ovens, extending across one third of the pastry bakehouse ceiling, was a huge smoke-hood shaped like a half-pyramid, designed to carry away all the smoke that issued from the oven mouths as they were fired up to temperature, just like those in the Outer Court bakehouse.

Unlike many of the other foods prepared in the kitchens, pastries could be kept fresh for quite a few days after being baked, so long as they remained cool and dry. For this reason, the north-facing room just to the east of the pastry was used as a dry larder (no. 28). Pre-empting modern food hygiene regulations by four and a half centuries, the Tudor cooks fully appreciated the need to keep raw and cooked foods separate if outbreaks of food-poisoning were to be avoided. By storing its finished goods here, the Pastry was able to maintain a reservoir of supplies ready to be whisked off down the Paved Passage to the servery hatches.

6

The Paved Passage

Larders, Boiling House, Workhouses

Between the Pastry Yard, the main kitchens and the Privy Orchard to the north lay a block of larders and preparation kitchens, all entered from a narrow central corridor open to the sky. Known as the Paved Passage up to the late seventeenth century at least, it is now called Fish Court (no. 27).

✿

The larder where the raw meat was stored was located at the centre of the Paved Passage's southern wall (no. 33). The meat delivered here was already butchered; the sergeant of the acatery who organised its transport on the hoof from the royal estates or the markets would have arranged the messy, noisy, smelly slaughtering well away from the main palace buildings. He and his officers took specified parts of each carcase as their fee: the sergeant received the head, tongue, midriff, paunch and four feet of each ox, while the yeoman and groom had its belly-piece, rump, and 'sticking-piece' along with the head, caul, 'gatherings' (heart, liver and lungs) and feet of each sheep; and the clerk got the head and skin of each veal calf.[1]

On arriving at the palace kitchens, the carcases would be brought through the Back Gate to the door leading from the Pastry Yard into the boiling house (no. 26) and from there into the larder. Here ventilation was very important for keeping the meat fresh, although the throughput must have been very rapid when the court was in residence. As Sir Hugh Plat advised, it was possible to 'keepe veale, mutton or venison in the heat of the summer 9 or ten daies good, so as it bee newly and faire killed, by

18. *The Paved Passage* Now known as 'Fish Court', this passageway provided the main means of communication between the larders, the boiling house, the pastry, the workhouses and the main kitchens. The upper rooms were used as lodgings for the staff who worked in the rooms directly below, the larder staff sleeping over the larders to the left.

hanging the same in an high and windie roome . . . this is an approved Secret easie and cheape, and very necessary to be knowne and practised in hote and tainting weather. Veale may be kept ten daies in bran.'[2] In the Larder, the meat was inspected by James Mitchell, sergeant of the larder, and its quantity recorded by his clerk, Anthony Weldon.[3] In 1541 Weldon had been granted both the income from the town of Penlosse in north-west Wales and the passage of boats to Conway, etc. By 1543 he was clerk of the pastry, and then promoted to second clerk of the kitchen, while in 1544, when he returned to the larder, he received the lease of the manor of Swanscombe in Kent. Weldon had done well for himself. But it was not unusual for officers to substantially improve their income through service in the household.[4]

The work cycle began here in the larder each evening, when the clerk comptroller and the clerk of the kitchen, together with the larder staff, attended 'the coupage of the fleyshe . . . in the grete larder, as requiryth nyghtly to knowe the proportion of beef and moton for the expences of the next day, and see the fees thereof, to be justly smytten by the yeoman cooke'.[5] The larder officers, like the acatery officers just mentioned, took their 'fees' in the form of joints cut off the ends of the carcases. The sergeant had the two joints of each ox cut from just above the rump, the two

19. *Larder fees* The ox and sheep heads, together with the tongue, as shown in this woodcut from Lobera de Avila's *Banket der Hofe und Edelleut* of 1556, would all have been cut off and taken as fees by the officers of the larder, leaving only the main carcases for the kitchens.

top neck joints with the 'bore of the head', the feet, the belly piece and the hindquarters 'to the arse bone', while the yeomen had the forelegs struck off at the first joint, and a piece of the first joint of the neck.[6] The yeomen also took three joints of the scrag-end of the necks of sheep and veal calves, along with their rumps and the lower parts of their back legs, while the grooms had the head, feet and small end of the chine, or lower back joint, of every hog. The main parts of the carcases, complete with ribs, breasts, shoulders, loins and hindquarters, would then be cut into portions, each sufficient to serve a certain number of messes 'according to the ancient custome'[7] Each ox, which would weigh some 500lb (227kg), was cut up into major joints that would provide the following messes:

	Messes
Two livery pieces	10
Two crops [necks]	6
Two briskets [lower chest]	6
Two sirloins [small of back]	4
Two shoulders	4
Chines (lower back)	4
Fillet (undercut to sirloin)	4
	38 messes

at 4 people per mess, 152 individual servings

As for the other carcases:

	Messes	*Individual servings*
One mutton	10	40
One veal	12	48
One pork	13	52
One stirk (a bullock or heifer of 1–2 years)	24	96

The meat was cut in the evening so as to be ready for cooking at any time after five the next morning, in time for the ten o'clock dinner. The poultry and rabbits that had been plucked or skinned in the scalding house in the Outer Court arrived in the larder before eight, so that the officers could distribute them to the various master cooks, as needed for that particular day's dinner and supper.

Just to the west of the larder lay the wet larder (no. 32), where the fresh fish was probably kept for almost immediate use. Most of the sea-fish was provided by Thomas Hewyt of Hythe in Kent, to whom a contract had

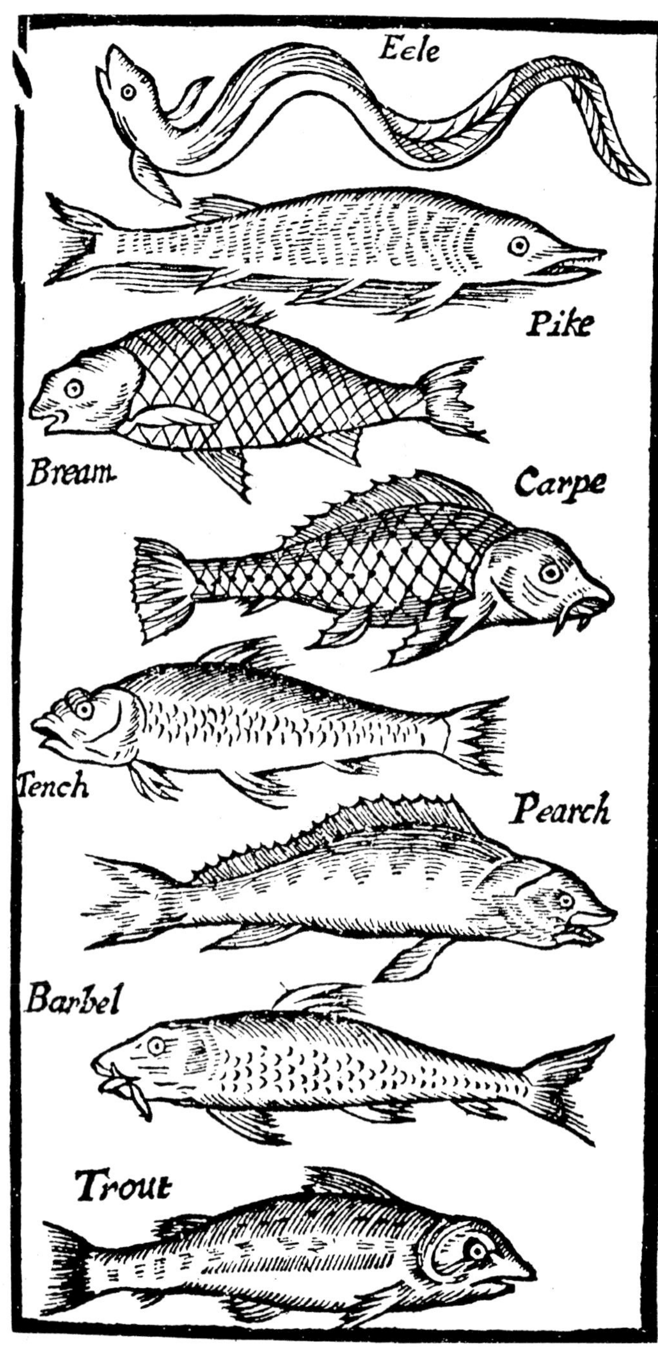

20. *Freshwater fish* Many of these varieties, illustrated in Hannah Woolley's *The Accomplish't Lady's Delight*, would have been brought into the larders shortly before being cooked on the Friday and Saturday fish-days.

been awarded by the officers of the greencloth.[8] He would send the fish up from the coast in panniers slung from the sides of pack-horses, led by a servant who also carried a note of its prices. The most expensive fish were bought individually, a halibut costing 2d, a John Dory 12d, and porpoises, not above one horseload, 13s 4d; the prices of larger ones were agreed with the clerks comptroller. The other fish were bought by the 'seam', a very practical measure since it represented a single horse-load:

1 seam of pilchards	6s
1 seam of herrings	9s
1 seam of mixed conger, cod, whiting and thornback	10s
if no conger or cod in seam	6s
1 seam of plaice	10s
1 seam of mullet, turbot and bass	13s

Freshwater fish was brought to the palace by purveyors such as Robert Parker and George Hill, who provided the following at these agreed rates:[9]

	Length	
pike, alive	18–21 in (46–53cm)	14d
bream	16–18 in (40–46cm)	30d
carp	16–18in (40–46cm)	48d
perch	9–12in (23–30cm)	3d
trout	14–17in (35–43cm)	8d
chub	16 in (40cm) or more	14d
roach, large	10in (25cm) or more	1d
roach, small	7–10in (17.5–2.5cm)	¼d
	Weight	
eels	3lb (1350g)	10d
panniers of crab and lobster	100lb (45kg)	96d
salmon, fresh and calver, by agreement with the clerk comptroller		

In addition, fish were kept in ponds extending from the front of the King's apartments at Hampton Court, across towards the Thames. These are now drained, but the site is still called the Pond Gardens.

Having been checked and recorded by the sergeant and clerk of the larder, the clerk of the kitchen and the clerk comptroller would presumably supervise the cutting of the 'fees' of the fish – for the master cooks had all the salmons' tails, the heads of turbot, halibut, purpoise and so forth.[10] The fish would then be given to the cooks so that they could prepare them for that day's meals.

❁

Next to the larder lay the boiling house (no. 26), staffed by four yeomen and two junior servants and supervised by the sergeant of the larder, who was charged to ensure that 'the Beef be put to the lead every morning in due time, soe that it may be thorough boyled when it shall be served'.[11] The 'lead' was a large metal cauldron permanently fixed into a masonry base or 'furnace'. In some establishments these vessels were made of brass: Dale Abbey in Derbyshire had 'a brasse pot in a furnes', and Barnwell Abbey in Cambridgeshire '1 great brass pott in a furneshe . . . 1 ladull; and a skomer [skimmer] of brass', for example.[12] Huge brass pots of this type are still be to be seen at Warwick Castle, and another at Laycock Abbey in Wiltshire bears an inscription stating that it was cast in 1500 by Peter Waghuens of Malines.

At Hampton Court a lead, or copper boiler, was installed in the boiling house in September 1531.[13] It was probably coated with tin inside, like the boiling vessels listed in the inventory of all equipment in the palace's kitchens drawn up for the Commonwealth in 1659, and like the copper pans used in any modern restaurant kitchen. (Without this tinning, the copper is attacked by the acids in the food, dissolving into it, spoiling the taste and eventually causing poisoning.) Early in the morning the lead would be filled with water – it probably had its own supply on tap from a cistern full of spring water in the rooms above. Faggots or similar fast-burning timber would then be lit and fed into the long firebox underneath, which had raised firebars to ensure that the fuel burned as fiercely as possible. From here the flames played directly on to the base of the copper and then were drawn up flues at the back of it and forwards around the upper parts of both sides, to ensure that they made maximum contact with the huge cauldron before being carried away up the chimney.

Although Hampton Court's original copper does not survive, the dimensions of the surrounding masonry and furnace arch show that it must have held around 80 gallons (364 litres), which would have given it the capacity to boil batches of around two hundred messes – enough to serve eight hundred people at a time. On the other hand, given that the household regulations state that its primary purpose was to boil all the beef, it would

21. *The Boiling House* This large built-in copper boiler was supplied with spring water from a tank in the rooms above, and was heated by a typical flue system which conducted the flames first underneath and then around its upper parts.

have been barely large enough to meet the demands placed upon it unless the better-quality beef for the nobles etc. was boiled in the Lord's side kitchen – as may have been the case.[14]

From its position, it looks as though the boiling house was used as a preparation facility for the pastry and main kitchens too. There would certainly have been time to receive the raw meats from the larder each night or early morning, parboil some of them between, say, 5 and 7.30 a.m. for transfer to the pastry for pie- and pasty-making, or to the kitchens for roasting, and still boil a batch of 200 two-pound (900g) beef joints ready for dinner at 10 a.m. Needless to say, the boiling house would have been constantly bustling, the staff busy non-stop with trimming and trussing the joints, putting them into the copper, stoking the fire, baling out the boiled meats into kettles and pans for transfer to the pastry, the other kitchens or the serving hatches. Then, once dinner had been served, they would start all over again so as to be ready for the four o'clock supper. For all this, in addition to their wages, the boiling house staff received the strippings from the brisket joints, the grease produced from the transfer of the meat from the boiler into the kettles and pans, and the dripping from the roasts in the kitchen.[15]

The major by-product of the boiling house was pottage. As the ever-informative Andrew Boorde recorded, 'Pottage is not so much used in al Crystendom as it is used in Englande. Potage is made of the lyquor in which flesshe is sodden [boiled] in, with puttyng-to chopped herbes and oatmeal and salt.'[16] It formed an excellent broth, as may be imagined from the following recipe:[17]

A GOOD POTTAGE

900g (2lb) rolled beef, brisket or lamb
8 spring onions
5ml (1tsp) salt
60ml (4 tbs) medium oatmeal
60ml (4 tbs) finely chopped herbs chosen from parsley, spinach, endive, strawberry leaves, violet leaves, succory (chicory) and marigold petals.

1. *Chop the onions, oatmeal and herbs very finely together.*
2. *Put the herb mixture into a deep saucepan half full of water, bring it to a rapid boil, stirring all the time, then put in the meat, ensuring that it is covered with the liquid.*
3. *Reduce the heat to a very gentle simmer, skim off the scum without removing the herbs, and leave to cook for 2 hours, stirring occasionally.*
5. *Just before serving the pottage – as a soup – stir in the salt. Then serve the boiled meat in a separate dish.*

All kinds of herbs were used for pottages – these were recommended by a cook who had contact with one of the King's sergeant cooks:[18]

All manner of herbs good for pottage

Take the crop of red brier,
Red nettle crop and avens [herb bennet, *Geum urbanum*] also
Primrose and violet together mostly go,
Lettuce, beets and borrage good,
Town cress, cress that speweth in flood,
Clary, savory, thyme good won,
Parsley worth other herbs many a one.
All other herbs thou not forsake,
But best of primrose thou shalt take,
Red cole [cabbage] half part pottage is,

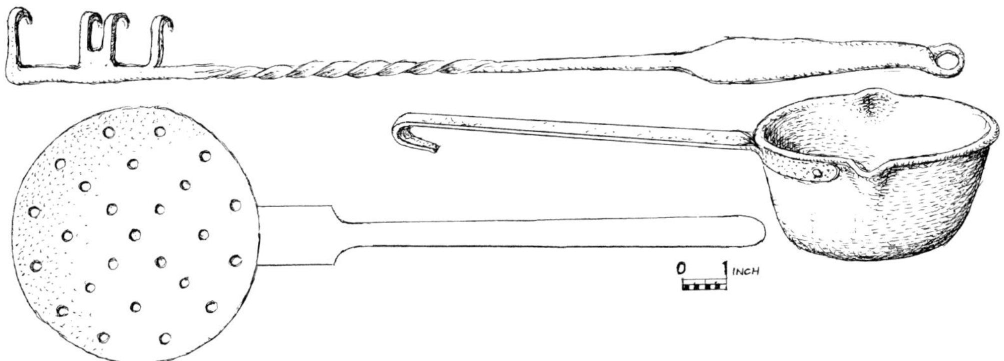

22. *Boiling utensils* The flesh hook was used to lift the hot meat out of the boiling water — this example was found in the cellar of a house in Norwich which burned down on 25 March 1507. The large broth ladle is based on one in Bartolommeo Scappi's famous cookery book of 1570, while the skimmer, for removing the scum, was used by William Coke, cook to William Cannynge of Bristol. When Coke was buried in his master's great church, St Mary Redcliffe, in 1467, the mason simply placed it on his gravestone and carved its outline, which remains there today.

From June to St James tide [25 July] I wis,
Then winter his course shall hold.
In lent season porray [leeks] be bold.

Such a range of flavourings to choose from, the juices given up by the meat and the smoothness of the gently simmered oatmeal made pottage an excellent start to any meal. It was also very practical from the cooks' point of view, since it required a minimum of attention during cooking and did not spoil if it was not served immediately. It was an excellent way of cooking mess-sized joints of meat, giving them a good flavour, and it enabled the cooks to boil two major dishes in a single pot. Furthermore, it provided those in the Great Hall and the Great Watching Chamber with a hot and filling dish to take the edges off their appetites as soon as they sat down at the tables.

On the opposite side of the Paved Passage, to the north between the dry larder and the main kitchens, were two rooms, each having a wide fireplace with a small oven set to one side of it (nos 30–31). In 1674 these were listed as the comptroller's and master of horse's kitchens, but this must be a later usage. From their position and their facilities, it is obvious that in the 1530s–40s they were the workhouses for the adjacent hall-place

ELEVATION
SECTION
PLAN
0 1 2 3 4 5 6 FT.

kitchen. These smaller kitchen workhouses were ideal for carrying out the more delicate cookery procedures, particularly the making of hot sauces which formed an integral part of many major dishes, and the better-quality small-scale roasting and baking. Unfortunately, there are neither inventories nor written descriptions to tell us how they were equipped and used. However, it is possible to make informed suggestions by comparing them with the contemporary commercial kitchens probably operating on a similar scale.

The ovens, for example, would be used exactly like those in the bakehouse and pastry and so could turn out dozens of small pastries and tarts. As for the fireplaces, they would appear to be unsuitable for full-scale roasting fires, particularly in view of the relatively small size of the rooms. Probably they would have had raised masonry hearths, where the cooking could take place at a convenient table-top height. As in the seventeenth to mid nineteenth century royal kitchens, they may have incorporated charcoal stoves. The seventeenth century charcoal stoves that still survive in the hall-place kitchen, presumably the very same that were used by great royal cooks such as Patrick Lamb, First Master Cook in the King's Kitchen from 1688 to 1709, perfectly illustrate their construction. Built of brick, they have a number of arched recesses set into their vertical fronts. Every other arch is simply a bunker for holding supplies of fresh charcoal, but the ones in between have square ducts going off to each side, each duct bridged by parallel rows of square wrought-iron firebars a few inches from the worktop. These form the bases of circular firepits, which held the burning charcoal. The fuel drew up a strong draught from below, while the ashes fell directly down into the empty arches beneath.

These stoves are far superior to any modern barbecue, burning efficiently with a steady, clear heat ideal for boiling or frying, and immeasurably more practical for undertaking the more delicate aspects of cookery than the great open hearths of the adjacent kitchens. They are very clean to use, too, their combustion gases leaving only a light coat of ash on the bases

23. *Charcoal stoves* These seventeenth century charcoal stoves (top) in the hall place kitchen are probably very similar to those used by the Tudor cooks. As the cross-section shows, three of the open arches have pairs of combined draught- and ash-holes serving the six fireplaces on the top, so that the fuel could burn with a clear, fierce heat. The other two arches formed convenient bunkers for fresh charcoal.

Hans Burgkmair's woodcut published in 1542 (bottom) shows a charcoal stove in use for boiling and broiling. Other interesting features include a chopping board with raised sides, cast-bronze cooking pots, a mortar and pestle and, to the right, a typical wooden salt-box with a sloping, hinged lid.

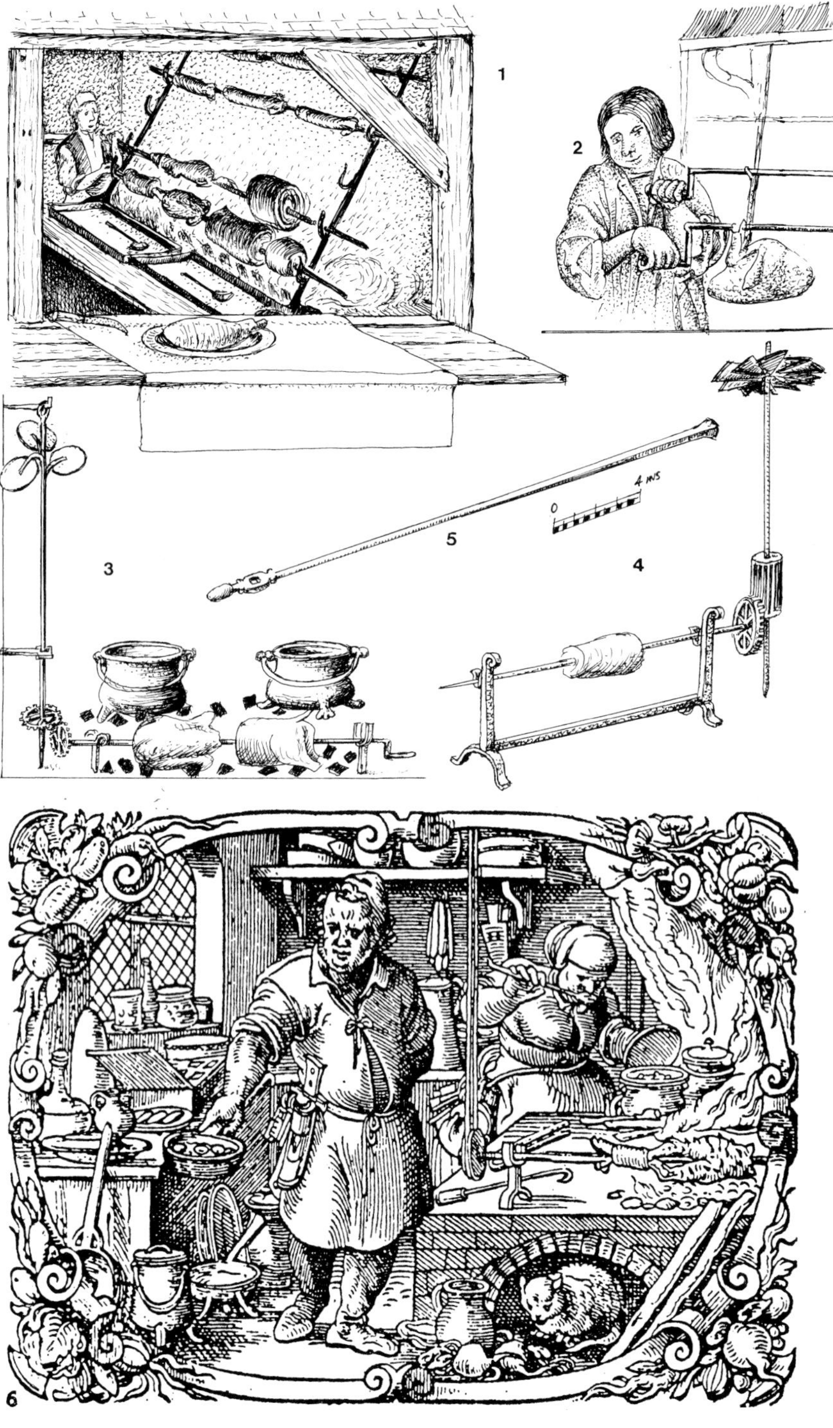
1
2
3
4
5
0
4 INS
6

of the cooking vessels, and producing no visible smoke. Under normal conditions, when the fumes are drawn straight upwards, these stoves present the cook with few problems, but when sudden draughts direct the invisible gases into his face the effects are devastating – rather like being punched on the nose by a scorching phantom boxing glove, leaving one gasping for breath, eyes watering and nostrils burning. Since the open top of each firepit was its effective chimney, pans could not be placed directly over it or the fire would be stifled. Instead, a triangular wrought-iron trivet with three legs a few inches high was used to support the cooking vessels; this also had the advantage of leaving the fire open to view, so that it could be poked to shake out the ash or have fresh charcoal added whenever necessary.

Raised masonry hearths were also used for roasting. The best illustration of this practice comes from Joris Hoefnagel's late sixteenth century painting, *The Marriage Feast at Bermondsey*, which shows a London cookshop in active use. A fire burns against the wall at the back of the masonry bench, and on either side is a cob-iron in the shape of an inverted T, its foot at the front of the bench and its shaft leaning back against the wall. This arrangement ensured that during their main cooking period the spits could be supported close to the fire at the bottom of the cob-irons, and then lifted away from the fire to rest in a cooler spot until the meat was ready to be served, while all the juices would be caught in rectangular dripping pans below.

In the *Bermondsey* painting, the spits are being turned by hand; a similar painting from Italy shows how the turnbroach, standing at one end, could operate two spits at once. Many northern European illustrations show the use of smoke-jacks on these raised roasting hearths: one end of the spit has a starting handle, while the other is linked by gears to a vertical shaft at the top of which is a large propeller. As the hot smoke and air rise up the chimney they turn the propeller, just like a windmill, which makes the spit turn in front of the fire. It was thought that these labour-saving devices were used solely on the Continent, but the excavation of

24. *High-level roasting* Town cook-shops used table-height roasting ranges, as seen in Hoefnagel's painting, *The Marriage Feast at Bermondsey* (1). Here the turnbroach operates two spits at once, like his late fifteenth century Italian counterpart at the Castello d'Issogne (2). Since this was the standard commercial practice of the period, it may have been adopted by cooks working in the royal household. They probably used jacks, too, like the one in drawing 3, based on a woodcut from *Kuchenmeisterei* (printed by Froschauer, Augsburg, 1507), and a drawing based on Bartolommeo Scappi's illustrations of 1570 (4). A jackshaft (5) was excavated from a cellar dated to 1507 in Norwich. The chicken roasting in the woodcut from Marx Rumpolt's *Ein Neu Kochbuch* of 1581 (6) is being turned by a rope driven from the smoke-jack in the chimney above.

the fan-shaft of one of these spits from a cellar in Norwich, filled with debris when the house above it burned down in 1507, has shown that they were used in England too and could therefore have been used in the Hampton Court kitchens.

With cooking facilities like these, along with all the smaller implements such as the graters, sieves, spice-boxes, salt-boxes, bowls, knives, spoons, skimmers, mixing bowls, cooking pots and frying pans, the palace cooks would be fully equipped to perform the tasks allotted them by the clerk of the kitchen.

7

The Hall-place and Lord's-side Kitchens

Boiling, Broiling, Roasting

At the east end of the Paved Passage lie the great kitchens – two huge rooms, each measuring forty feet (12m) up to the ridge of their arch-braced wooden roofs. These are the most impressive rooms in the whole suite of kitchen offices, and provide ample visual evidence of the importance of the kitchens within the royal household.

In England, cooks in great households have always had a reputation for being hot-tempered and irascible and for employing a memorable vocabulary and turn of phrase – a tradition that has been perpetuated unabated in the persons of many of their modern-day equivalents in the hotel and restaurant business. But considering the quality and volume of the dishes they have to prepare, the need for unfailing punctuality, and the constant heat and bustle of the kitchens where unforeseen accidents and ineptitude are part of the daily pattern, this is hardly surprising. John Earle's description, in his *Microcosmagraphie* of 1628, captures the man:[1]

> The kitchen is his hell, and he the devil in it, where his meat and he fry together. His revenues are showered down from the fat of the land, and he interlards his own grease among to help the drippings. Choleric he is, not by nature so much as his art, and it is a shrewd temptation that the chopping knife is so near. His weapons of war offensive are a mess of hot broth and scalding water, and woe be to him that comes in his way. In the kitchen he will domineer and rule the roast, in spite of his master, and curses is the very dialect of his calling. His labour

> is mere blustering and fury, and his speech like that of sailors in a storm, a thousand businesses at once; yet in all this tumult he does not love combustion, but will be the first man that shall go and quench it. He is never good Christian till a hissing pot of ale has slaked him, like water cast on a firebrand, and for that time he is tame and dispossessed . . . He is a pitiless murderer of innocents, and he mangles poor fowls with unheard of torchures, and it is thought the martyr's persecutions were devised from hence; sure we are Saint Lawrence his gridiron came out of his kitchen. His best facility is at the dresser, where he seems to have great skill in the tactics, ranging his dishes in order military and placing with great discretion in the fore-front meats more strong and hardy, and the more cold and cowardly in the rear, as quaking tarts, and quivering custards, and such milk-sop dishes which scape many times the fury of the encounter. But now the second course is gone up, and he down into the cellar; where he drinks and sleeps till four o'clock in the afternoon, and then returns again to his regiment.

The chief cook in the royal household was John Bricket. Although he was entitled 'the King's master cook', his responsibilities extended far beyond the King's Privy Kitchen to embrace the operation of the whole kitchen complex, from the larder doors through to the dresser hatches where the food was despatched to the dining areas. He was a man of considerable importance: the King granted him the stewardship of Caversham in Oxfordshire and an annuity for life from the issues (tax income) of the counties of Cheshire and Flint, in addition to his wages.[2]

Along with his other duties, he had to get rid of all 'corruption and uncleanesse . . . which doth ingender infection, and is very noisome and displeasant unto all noblemen and others' coming to court.[3] More especially he had to prevent the scullions, or junior kitchen staff, from going 'naked or in garments of such vilenesse as they now doe, and have been accustomed to doe, nor lie in the nights and dayes in the kitchens or ground by the fire-side'. From 1530, such practices – which must surely have befouled the kitchens and everything that passed through them – were banned. From now on the scullions had to be selected from candidates who might reasonably be expected to become cooks, and they were trained with this in mind. Instead of sleeping warm and cosy by the fireside, they were probably sent up to the garrets over the rooms to the north of the Paved Passage – quarters that I know from personal experience would be freezing cold in winter, and therefore probably very unpopular! In addition, the master cook was now issued with a sum of money each year for providing the scullions with 'honest and whole coarse garments', which were to be kept so clean that their appearance would never cause offence. In 1541, he was given £50 'for appareling of 33 galapines [scullions] for one year fully to be run at Christmas next coming'.[4]

The palace's perceptive management policies extended to making sure that not only were the kitchen staff always supplied with clean and adequate clothing, and personally clean, but that, by making them clean up the courtyards and passages around the palace, they also had the opportunity for some healthy outdoor exercise. The household ordinances instructed that the 'said scullions, a certain number alternately to be deputed, shall daily, once in the forenoone and once in the afternoone, sweepe and make cleane the courts, outward galleryes, and other places of the court, so there remaine no filfth or uncleannesse in the same', to the satisfaction of the sergeant of the hall. The sum of £55 allotted for 33 such 'galapines' shows that they received each year clothing costing, on average, £1 13s 4d each. In contrast Pero Doulx, the French yeoman cook for the King's mouth, received six times as much – £10 a year – for his clothing, in addition to his wages of £13 16s 8d, reflecting his much higher status.[5]

Most of the kitchen staff appear to have been relatively well dressed, as they are depicted in the painting of *The Field of the Cloth of Gold* of around 1545; only men were employed here due to the numerous dirty and laborious duties they had to perform, and their role as potential soldiers to defend the King. Along with all their contemporaries, they would have worn short, close-fitting linen braies, or underpants, secured by a drawstring at the waist. Over this came a plain white linen shirt, the main part made from a single length of cloth, folded end to end and seamed down the sides; a T-shaped cut would have been made on the fold to form the collar and front opening, and the sleeves, sewn on separately, would be wide enough to be rolled up for working. In accordance with sumptuary laws, the shirt would have neither the gathering nor the embroidery that distinguished the aristocratic shirts of this period. Since the kitchen staff usually worked in their shirtsleeves, the sleeves of their black or buff-coloured woollen doublets extended no further than half-way down the upper arm, some boldly puffed in accordance with contemporary fashion. They wore close-fitting, thigh-length hose, cut on the bias from red or white woollen cloth and seamed down the calf. Above these came the upper stocks, or trunk-hose – lined woollen breeches puffed and slashed at the knee and thigh. These would be held up by laces or 'points', threaded through corresponding pairs of holes in the waistband of the trunk-hose and the hem of the doublet, neatly knotted but leaving sufficient slack for freedom of movement, particularly at the rear. A black woollen hat and a pair of broad-toed leather shoes, cut very low at the instep, completed their everyday dress.

Over this, to keep themselves clean and tidy, the cooks wore white linen aprons, which were fairly short and wide in comparison to those worn today. The quality of the fabric varied according to the status of the wearer. Presumably they were very similar to those worn by the junior staff in the Counting House, where on the four great feasts of the year the sergeant received 7 feet 6 inches (2.3 metres) of linen costing about 9½d a yard, the yeomen 3 feet 9 inches (1.1 metres) costing about 6½d a yard, and the groom the same amount at 5d a yard.[6] If it came in 18-inch (46cm) widths, this would make up a pair of aprons nearly two feet (60cm) wide and a foot and a half (46cm) deep, which would look similar to those worn by the cooks in sixteenth-century illustrations.

Although the administrators of Henry VIII's household left ample documentary evidence of their activities, his cooks left virtually none. They were certainly very experienced professionals: the written descriptions of the great feasts they prepared show that they were capable of achieving the highest of international standards. To give us some impression of the hall-place and Lord's-side cookery, we have only two sources, neither of which is anywhere near as complete as we might wish. The first is the 'dietary' of the court, which forms part of the household ordinances.[7] It lists the dishes served to each division of the household, and sometimes gives brief details of the way they were cooked. The second is the body of high-class recipes published in England from the later sixteenth century.

Although much research remains to be done on this subject, it would appear that most of these recipes originated in the royal kitchens. Following the Dissolution, the granting of former monastic lands to influential families brought them increased wealth, and with this came the means to leave their country retreats and flood into London. Here men saw the chance to gain further wealth and advancement through contacts at court and at such institutions as the Inns of Court. While they spent the bulk of their day pursuing such interests, their ladies took the opportunity to develop their social and culinary skills, which on returning home they could proudly demonstrate to their less fortunate country cousins and neighbours. As Lucy Aitken recorded in her *Memoirs of the Court of Queen Elizabeth*, published in 1819:[8]

25. *The Hall-place Kitchen* Built for Henry VIII about 1530, this kitchen prepared all the food for the lesser courtiers and household officers who dined in the Great Hall. Raw food came in from the larders at the end, was cooked in the fireplaces, then served through the hatches in the left-hand wall.

> Many of the elder sort of courtier ladies were also skilful in surgery and the distillation of waters . . . each of them cunning in something whereby they keep themselves occupied in the court . . . when they be at home [they] can help supply the ordinary want of the kitchen with a number of delicate dishes of their own devising, wherein the portingal [Portuguese] is their chief counsellor, as some of them are most commonly with the clerk of the kitchen.

In this way the Elizabethan ladies learned the royal recipes and then spread them around the country – so effectively, indeed, that dishes such as the baked egg custards, which hitherto appeared only in the dietaries for the King and Queen, soon began to rapidly descend the social scale and can still be found in bakers' shops in many parts of England.

As the interest in fine cookery began to grow among the wives of the nobility and gentry, publishers started to produce books for the new market. Up to this time England had managed to publish only three cookery books, *The Boke of Cokery* about 1500, *A proper newe Booke of Cokerye* sometime before 1545, and the English translation of Alexis of Piedmont's *Secrets* in 1562. To these were now added John Partridge's *The Treasurie of Commodious Conceits and Hidden Secrets* (1573), A.W.'s *A Booke of Cookry Very Necessary for All Such as Delight Therein* (1584), Thomas Dawson's *The Good huswife's Jewell* (1587), and the anonymous *A Closet for Ladies & Gentlewomen* (1608). Gervase Markham's *The English Huswife* of 1615, printed from a manuscript written some time earlier by 'an honourable Personage of this kingdome', perhaps one of those ladies described by Lucy Aitken, contained similar material.

It is to these books that we must turn to discover how food was cooked in Henry VIII's kitchens, rather than to the late fourteenth century recipes of Richard II's cooks (now splendidly edited by Constance Hieatt and Sharon Butler as *Curye on Inglysch*[9] which were largely out of date by this period. Unlike many historical sources, early printed recipe books usually inform us of what was new and fashionable a generation or two before their date of publication, rather than what was just being introduced. As a typical example, we can read in Robert May's *The Accomplish't Cook*, published in 1660, how the confectionery castles and ships of the Tudor period were actually served – one positioned at each end of a long table, blasting each other with sweetmeat cannon charged with real gunpowder, while piecrusts containing live blackbirds were opened to add to the joyous confusion, making 'the Ladies to skip and shreek'. May had been apprenticed about 1607 to the cook to the Court of the Star Chamber, a royal institution which had always provided itself with the finest of dinners, and so, writing many years later, he was still able to publish recipes of Elizabethan or earlier origin, from those lamented days before 'good housekeeping left *England*'.[10]

At Hampton Court and at the other royal residences three different qualities and ranges of food had to be prepared for three different groups of people, and so the kitchens were divided into three separate units. The hall-place kitchen cooked for the minor courtiers and household servants who dined in the main body of the Great Hall; the Lord's-side kitchen cooked for the nobles and senior household servants who dined on the dais in the Great Hall, in the Council Chamber, in the Great Watching Chamber or in their own offices; and the Privy Kitchen cooked for the King and Queen. This arrangement ensured the maximum efficiency, enabling the clerk of the kitchen to allocate food from the larders to the appropriate kitchen, where the sergeant, yeoman and groom cooks, the scullions and turn-broaches, could develop their distinctive recipes and expertise.

The hall-place kitchen (no. 39), the first kitchen you come to at the end of the Paved Passage, occupies part of the site of Wolsey's hall-place kitchen-workhouse – its eastern end and the eastern half of the south wall survive from this building. The remainder was demolished and rebuilt in a greatly extended form for Henry VIII in 1529–31, to create a massive rectangular kitchen measuring almost fifty feet (15m) by thirty feet (9m), with walls twenty-three feet (7m) high to the eaves. This room was certainly not designed for delicate cookery; it was, in essence, a great boiling and roasting kitchen, ideally suited for mass catering on the largest scale. Its huge capacity is clearly demonstrated by the size of the great fireplaces. There are three of them, each some eighteen feet (5.5m) wide, six feet (1.8m) deep, and seven feet (2.1m) high. Their broad Tudor arches, cut from great blocks of stone, are quite narrow from front to back so as to help prevent the escape of smoke, but the brickwork above is considerably thicker and incorporates relieving arches which transfer the great weight of the chimney-stacks away from the masonry arches down to the sturdy side walls. Unlike most Georgian and later kitchen fireplaces – which, since they were designed to produce mainly radiant heat for roasting, were much shallower – those at Hampton Court are very deep. Their six-foot (1.8m) depth was necessary to create the very large working hearth area, in total some 324 square feet (30 square metres) in this kitchen alone, on which a number of separate fires and cooking processes could be in operation simultaneously. Quite different from later cooking methods, it was none the less a very flexible and practical system.

All the fireplaces burned wood in the form of large logs or talshides. Manoeuvring tons of this heavy, bulky material in through the Back Gate, through the Boiling House and along the Paved Passage would have been an extremely awkward business, bringing unwelcome dirt, labourers and congestion into an already bustling environment. For this reason, a wide archway had been built in the orchard wall at the north side of the Back Gate, and similar ones in the eastern end of the north wall and in the centre of the west well of the adjacent Lord's-side kitchen, so as to provide a convenient direct route to the fireplaces from the woodyard in the Outer Court. These archways also served another important purpose. Fires need both fuel and a good supply of fresh air, if they are to burn efficiently. Once the brickwork of the huge chimney-stacks had warmed up, they drew up vast quantities of hot air and smoke from the logs flaming on the hearths below, thoroughly ventilating the kitchen with their strong draught. In summertime this greatly improved the working conditions. But in winter, when the kitchens were almost permanently in the shadow of the Great Hall, it turned these rooms into the iciest of wind-tunnels. Frost and dustings of snow would remain unmelted for days on the window-ledges and pointing of their north façade, and inside, despite the roaring fires, the cooks may well have worked for days at a time in sub-zero temperatures. This was vividly brought home to me over Christmas and New Year of 1996–7, when the weather was so cold that the Thames froze over. While I was working here one clear, cloudless day, flurries of snow began to fall across the kitchen tables and floor. But these had not been blown in through the roof, which is completely weathertight – they were formed when the water vapour rising from the cooking pots simmering on the stoves froze in the chill air of the roofspace above and then descended as snowflakes!

To carry out cooking operations within the Hampton Court kitchen fireplaces, the cooks must have had access to a substantial *batterie de cuisine*. No contemporary descriptions survive, but it is probable that the original pieces of equipment, along with various replacements, were included in the parliamentary survey of the kitchen undertaken in 1659. Copper and brass cooking pots can enjoy a very long working life; some pieces acquired by certain country houses in the 1820s were still in use up to the 1940s, for example, while one down-hearth frying pan removed from the kitchens of Cowdray House in Sussex in 1793 was apparently used by a local family before being returned, still in good condition, some 150 years later. The 1659 inventory includes:

For boiling 1 copper to boil meat in, covered with lead (this would be the built-in copper in the Lord's-side

	kitchen boiling house)
	6 very large copper pots, tinned
	2 smaller ones, tinned
	5 brass kettles with iron feet, tinned
(fish)	2 great copper cans to boil fish in
	1 large long copper with a false bottom to boil fish in
	5 large brass pieces with holes in them to take fish out of the pans
(pudding)	4 pudding pans
(storing)	6 storing pans of copper, tinned
(equipment)	3 iron trivets
	3 brass scummers and a brass ladle
For roasting	9 spits
	1 pair of large iron racks (presumably those still there)
	4 large iron dripping pans
For broiling	2 very large gridirons
For frying	3 great frying pans
Miscellaneous	11 flat brass dishes, tinned over
	18 wooden trays
	5 cleavers or chopping knives

Some of these items would have been used in the hall-place kitchen, where a fairly limited range of foods was cooked – mainly boiled, probably – beef, mutton, lamb, veal, coney and goose on meat days, and ling, plaice, whiting and other 'sea-fish' on fish days. From contemporary illustrations and excavated examples we can gain a good impression of the appearance and construction of the tinned copper pots: their bases raised from thick sheet metal, their sides extended with riveted plates, and their rims wire-edged around thick wrought-iron hoops, with stout suspension rings at each side. They would have been filled with meat, water and seasonings, and then placed on iron trivets in the fireplaces. A full boiling pot might easily have weighed a quarter of a ton (254kg) or even considerably more – a weight that could not be managed without the help of machinery. The Prince Regent's cooks used a crane with a block-and-tackle to raise their much smaller tinned copper pots on to the stoves in the kitchens of Windsor Castle.[11] Most probably their Tudor predecessors used devices such as those illustrated by their Italian contemporary Bartolommeo Scappi. His first major job was probably as cook to Cardinal Campeggio, the papal Legate who handled the negotiations over the divorce of Henry VIII and Catherine of Aragon, but then he went on to be cook to Popes Pius IV and Pius V.

26. *Cauldrons* Massive copper cauldrons were essential for boiling, these examples including one excavated from a Dutch ship wrecked in 1597 (1) another by Giacomo Valesio (1548–87) (2), and three illustrated by Bartolommeo Scappi in 1570: his fish kettle (4) was cut away to show its internal drainer, while his large boiling cauldron (5), weighing around a quarter of a ton (254 kg), is depicted with its special lifting gear. In the Tudor royal kitchens, some of the cauldrons were much broader, as seen in the painting of *The Field of the Cloth of Gold* (6). Note the stirring paddle lying on the ground.

The magnificent cookery book *Opera*, which he published in 1570, includes over a thousand recipes for some of the finest food in Europe, as well as a unique series of engravings of all manner of kitchen equipment. One of these shows the cooks taking a great boiling pot off the fire using a platform mounted on four small wheels, across the middle of which rises a rectangular frame rather like extended goal-posts. By placing a long lever over the top of this, they were able to hook one end on to the handle of the pot, loop the other end under a hook attached to a drawbridge-like extension at the back of the platform, and with a combination of their own strength and body weight lift the pot and manoeuvre it into position over the fire. The pot's open top would then usually be covered with a lid; if left open, smoke would have swirled down on to the surface of the boiling liquid, contaminating its flavour and combining with its fats to create a foul black mess with the density and stickiness of printer's ink.

It is possible that the cooks followed the international peasant practice of maintaining what Alexandre Dumas called 'the eternal kettle'.[12] The eternal kettle is – or rather, was, since this illustrious gastronomic institution long ceased to function – a receptacle that never left the fire, day or night. As a chicken was taken out of it another was put in, as a piece of beef was taken out, another would take its place; a glass of water would be added whenever a cup of broth was removed. Every kind of meat that cooked in this bouillon gained rather than lost in flavour, for it inherited the juices provided by all the meat that preceded it and in turn bequeathed some of its own. It was not necessary to leave the meat in the kettle any longer than it required to cook, so it lost none of its qualities.

A few years ago I was able to gain detailed information about this method of cookery from a man who had seen it still being practised in the heart of the North York Moors about the time of the First World War, and later I was able to put it to the test there by cooking all my food in a cauldron over an open fire for two weeks. In this region, the pot was taken off the fire every evening, so that in the morning when it was cold, all the congealed fat was carefully skimmed off, the pot placed over the fire, fresh water added until it was half full, and all the scum skimmed off immediately it came to the boil. The meat, such as fresh beef or mutton or a trussed chicken, was then put in, each at the appropriate time, so as to be just ready for the required meal, and left to barely simmer. About an hour before they were to be served, the larger whole scrubbed vegetables were added, their unbroken skins ensuring that they retained virtually all their original flavour as they cooked. (Alternatively, the smaller vegetables such as peas and beans, and the larger chopped ones, can be put in a little later, having first put them in a thin cloth or a string bag). Neither salt nor spices were put in, though, because their flavours would accumulate and spoil the stock. When the meal was ready, some of the stock was simply ladled out into a dish as a first course, then the meat and vegetables withdrawn a little later for the main course. After this the skimmer was used to remove every particle of solid food from the pot, and it was set aside in a cool place until required again, unless needed to prepare the second meal of the day. Since the stock was boiled for two or three hours every day, and contained no cereals or other solid matter at any other time, it always remained perfectly sweet, its flavour improving in richness and quality as the days passed. This very practical method would certainly have been suitable for use in the kitchens of Hampton Court.

Joints of meat were also cooked in pottages, as we saw earlier in the recipe for 'A Good Pottage' (p. 104). The following recipe was ideal for large-scale catering, since it required the minimum of preparation and was suitable for all red meats:[13]

POTTAGE WITH WHOLE HERBS

900g (2lb) joint of mutton, lamb or beef
100g (4oz) each of the whole leaves of lettuce, spinach, endive, and white cabbage or cauliflower
5–10ml (1–2 tsp) salt
60ml (4 tbs) wine vinegar
50g (2oz) fine or medium oatmeal
3 English onions, sliced
small squares or triangles of white bread

1. *Half fill a large cooking pot with water, bring it to the boil, plunge in the meat, and remove the scum as it rises. Then reduce the heat to a gentle simmer.*
2. *Mix the oatmeal with 275ml (½ pt) cold water, and stir it into the pot.*
3. *Add the vegetables, and continue simmering for 1½ hours, until the meat is tender. Then add the salt and wine vinegar.*
4. *Lift the meat out on to a dish, lift out the vegetables with a skimmer, lay them on top, and decorate the edges with the pieces of bread. Then keep warm until the remaining stock has been served first as a pottage.*

Before serving pottages such as this, the cooks tasted them, and then modified their flavours, using ingredients such as these, suggested by Gervase Markham:

TO CORRECT THE FLAVOUR OF BROTHS[14]

When a broth is too sweet, sharpen it with verjuice [use wine vinegar], when it is too tart, sweet it with sugar, when flat and wallowish, quicken it with oranges and lemons, and when it is too bitter, make it pleasant with herbs.

Coneys, which we would now call rabbits, formed a very cheap and plentiful food for the Great Hall at a time when it was 'not at all uncommon to see at one time an hundred rabbits running about in one meadow'. Having been skinned and 'paunched' (drawn) in the Poultry, they were made into a rich and flavoursome large-scale stew:[15]

SMOTHERED RABBITS

4 rabbits
1800g (4lb) onions
100g (4oz) currants
white bread cut in 2.5cm (1in cubes)
1.7l (3pt) water
100g (4oz) butter
2.5ml (½ tsp) salt
1.5ml (¼ tsp) pepper
150ml (¼pt) cider vinegar

1. *Clean and joint the rabbits and rub them with the salt and pepper.*
2. *Peel and quarter the onions, put them into a pot with the remaining ingredients except the bread, and simmer for 1½ hours, until the rabbit is cooked.*
3. *Arrange the bread in the bottom of a dish, lay the rabbit joints on top, then pour their juices over them.*

Vegetables would also have been boiled in the hall-place kitchen, probably using very simple recipes such as this:[16]

BUTTERED WORTS

A selection of 'pot herbs' such as red or white cabbage, carrots, lettuce, leeks and onions all coarsely chopped
butter
salt
2.5cm (1in) cubes of bread

1. *To each 450 (1lb) of vegetables allow 50g (2oz) of butter. Melt the butter in a stewpan and heat it gently without allowing it to colour, skimming off any scum. Remove it from the heat, allow to cool a little, then pour the clear butter into a large saucepan.*

2. *Add the vegetables to the saucepan, almost cover them with water, boil for 20–30 minutes until they are tender, and only then add salt to taste.*
3. *Spread the bread cubes across the base of a deep dish, ladle the vegetables on top, then pour in enough of the buttery stock to fill the dish.*

In this kitchen, the boiled fish was cooked in large, shallow tinned copper pots with removable false bottoms or drainers, as described in the inventory of 1659. They would be set up over a gentle fire on iron trivets, then filled with stock such as the one described in this recipe:[17]

TO BOIL FISH

A small bundle of rosemary and thyme, bound together, and a few sprigs of parsley
5ml (1 tsp) salt
850ml (1½ pt) water
25g (1oz) butter
15g (½oz) fresh yeast (or dried equivalent)

27. *Cooking fish* Most of the fish required for dinners and suppers every Friday and Saturday was broiled over glowing embers on large gridirons, or simmered in herb-flavoured stock in fish kettles.

Simmer all the ingredients together for 10–15 minutes, then put in the fish, and cook until tender (plaice and whiting take about 10 minutes).

TO DRESS SALT LING[18]

pieces of dry salted ling	water

1. Soak the ling overnight in cold water.
2. Put it into a pan of fresh water, then bring it to the boil and continue cooking for 1½ hours.
3. Let the water cool enough so that the fish can be handled, remove it from the pan, pick out the loose bones and scrape the skin clean without removing it.
4. Put the fish into a fresh pan of boiling water and cook for a further 1½ hours.

To make a higher-quality dish, the cooked ling had the following sauce poured over it:[19]

STOCKFISH SAUCE

575ml (1pt) eel, pike or salmon stock, strained	15ml (1 tbs) fresh parsley, finely chopped
15ml (1 tbs) wine vinegar	1.5ml (½ tsp) ground ginger

Simmer these together for 10–15 minutes, then pour the stock over the fish just before serving.

The other large-scale method of cooking fish was to broil it, placing it on one of the very large gridirons, supported a few inches above a level mass of glowing embers. Gridirons of this type are to be seen hanging against the wall in A. Pugin's early-nineteenth-century view of the kitchens of Christ Church, Oxford: each gridiron was some three feet (90cm) square, with parallel rows of iron bars on which to place the fish. This was a fairly rapid method of cooking:[20]

TO BROIL FISH

450g (1lb) fresh fish, such as sole, plaice, mackerel or herring, or steaks or fillets of larger fish	25g (1oz) butter 60ml (4 tbs) wine vinegar 1.5ml (¼ tsp) ground black pepper

1. Melt and beat the butter, vinegar and pepper together to form a hot sauce.
2. Cook the fish over a barbecue or under a grill for 2 minutes on each side, turning them from time to time and removing them further from the heat if they are cooking too quickly. If using a barbecue, place the grid at a slight angle, so that the fish juices run down along the bars rather than dropping into the fire to send up plumes of fine ash. The cooking times will be about: 1.3cm (½in) thickness, 7–8 minutes; 2.5cm (1in) thickness, 10 minutes; 4cm (1½in) thickness, 15–18 minutes.

Most fish, except salmon or eel, were also fried in unsalted or clarified butter, or olive oil, after being dipped into milk and then floured (or just floured), before being placed into the hot fat. Fresh parsley was fried in the same pan immediately after the fish had been removed, and then laid over it ready for serving.[21]

Roasting was primarily a method reserved for cooking the more tender joints of meat, along with poultry and game. Today the word 'roast' is almost always used to mean baked. It might seem unnecessary to differentiate between these two words, but they are in fact distinct methods of cookery, and produce quite different results. When a joint is 'roasted' in the modern sense in an oven, it is enclosed within a small volume of static, or virtually static air, and sits in a tin of boiling fat and juices which frequently scorch to blackness around the sides. The whole atmosphere inside the oven becomes heavy and fat-laden, carrying the odour of the overcooked fats, which may then permeate the meat, giving it a fairly heavy flavour. Real roasting, in contrast, relies solely on a fierce radiant heat: the meat is mounted on a spit where it remains constantly suspended in a stream of fresh air that carries off all unwanted smells and leaves any excess fats free to drop away, thus rendering the meat light and flavoursome.

The equipment for roasting, as listed in the 1659 inventory, comprised spits, racks and dripping pans, all of which are shown in use in the painting of *The Field of the Cloth of Gold*, where a roasting hearth is set up in just the same way as the remaining roasting hearth in the Lord's-side kitchen at Hampton Court. In order to contain the fire, two nine-inch (23cm) English-bond walls were built six feet (1.8m) apart in the middle of the fireplace, each with its front face sloping back at 20° from the vertical. These served as supports for two great wrought-iron racks, or cob-irons, each with a wide horizontal foot to keep it upright, and eight projecting bars with semicircular notches cut into their upper edges to receive the spits or 'broches'. In this way any spit could be securely rotated

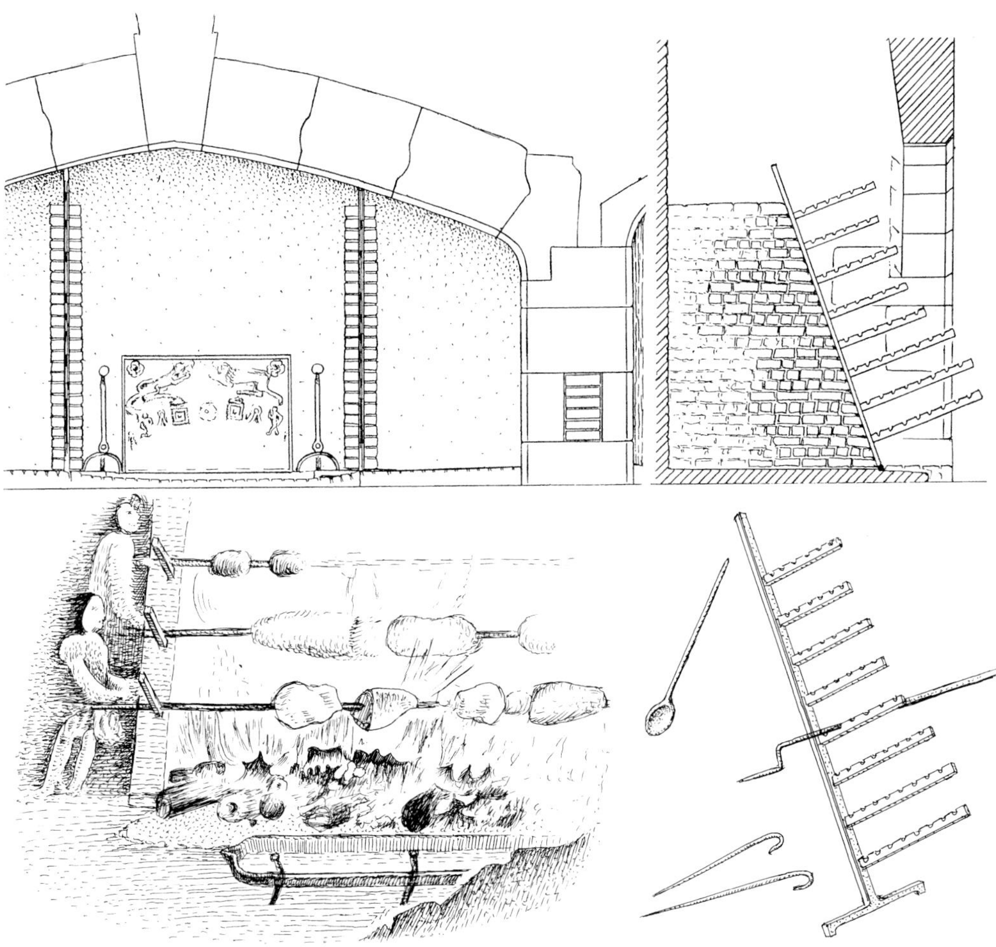

28. *Roasting* The great racks or cob-irons in the Lord's-side kitchen fireplace probably date from around 1530; they were set up exactly as shown in the painting of *The Field of the Cloth of Gold*, and were also recorded at Hampton Court in the seventeenth century. Note the dripping pan which caught the juices, the skewers used for trussing and the spoon for basting the meat.

in any one of fifty-four different positions. Since the spits had to bridge six feet nine inches (2.1m) between the two racks and had to carry substantial moving weights, they needed to be at least one inch (2.5cm) square in cross-section and over nine feet (2.7m) in length. Those spits shown in contemporary continental paintings, as well as early examples in museum collections, usually have rectangular-cross-sectioned central working lengths, sometimes with holes punched through them at regular intervals. These features demonstrate an attempt to overcome one of the main problems with spit cookery: it is easy enough to slide a piece of meat on to the pointed end of a spit but quite another to keep it rotating, because its natural tendency is to hang still while the spit rotates uselessly inside it. The rectangular section helped to prevent this, especially if the meat was secured with a pair of skewers passing tight across each broad side of the spit, and if another was stuck through both the joint and one of the holes in the spit the process was further aided and accelerated. The alternative method, using 'dogs' – forked brackets that slid along the spit to impale the joint on its sharp prongs – appears to have been introduced at a later date.

The actual turning of the spit was a simple manual operation. With one person sitting and another standing behind him, both protected from the heat behind the sloping wall and turning a spit with each hand, four spits could be operated from one side; this meant that twenty-four feet (7.3m) of spit could be in continuous use, with room on the upper bars to hold the roasted joints in the gentler heat before being served. It may even have been possible to double this capacity if another four spits were turned from the opposite side. Spit-turning had to be done at a steady pace, so that the surface of the meat closest to the fire could absorb a body of heat without burning, while allowing the heat to be absorbed into the joint during the rest of the rotation. It was important, too, to keep the meat at a sufficient distance from the fire – if it was too close it scorched on the outside, which prevented the heat from penetrating further. As Thomas Tusser stated:[22]

> Good diligent turn-broche and trusty withall,
> Is sometimes as needfull as some in the hall.

In addition to turning the meat, it was also necessary to 'froth' and baste it to keep in the flavour and moisture. As later authors tell us, beef, mutton and goose, the principal meats to be roasted in the Hall-place kitchen, were first basted with a little salt and water from the dripping pan, the shallow trough placed beneath the spits to catch the juices. Once this had dried, the meat was dredged with flour, and then basted with butter to create a thin crust or froth all over the outside. This was quite unlike the usual continental method, which involved inserting strips of fat bacon or 'lard' across the surface of the meat – one contemporary visitor to England observed that 'in this country the men, as well nobles as traders and husbandmen, never lard their meat, but only anoint it with butter'.[23]

While these basic operations were being carried out in the Hall-place kitchen, similar activities using a better quality and range of ingredients, and more elaborate techniques, were taking place in the Lord's-side kitchen (no. 41). This had been built as Cardinal Wolsey's household kitchen sometime after he had obtained the lease of Hampton Court in 1514. Its 39- by 28-foot (11.9 x 8.5m) floor space and three large fireplaces were large enough to serve his household of about five hundred, but totally inadequate to cater for the court of Henry VIII. From around 1530 it therefore became the 'Lord's-side kitchen', cooking for those who dined on the dais of the Great Hall and in the Great Watching Chamber. The only major alteration at this period of transition was the rebuilding of the arch of the north fireplace, reducing its width from some 18 feet (5.5m) to 15 feet (4.6m). No culinary requirement would make this necessary, and so it may have been done for structural reasons, particularly if the wider arch had showed signs of failing. Wolsey's boiling house, set in a small room off the north-west corner of this kitchen, was retained intact, so that it could provide similar facilities to those in the boiling house back in the Paved Passage.

Just as the hall-place kitchen had its smaller kitchen-workhouses in which the more delicate cookery tasks were carried out, the Lord's-side kitchen had its own equivalent (no. 45). It was a single room located some twenty feet (6.1m) to the east of this kitchen, at the opposite side of the large servery area called the Great Space (no. 44). It measured about twenty feet (6.1m) square, with a wide fireplace arch in its south wall suitable for either a stove or a raised roasting hearth, and had a dresser hatch cut through its west wall. Its size and location suggest that it had been built as Cardinal Wolsey's privy kitchen, where the finest food was prepared for him and his chief guests. It may have been one of the first structures he built here, for an account of 1515 mentions 'red okre for the chymny of the prevey kitchin'.[24]

In the Lord's-side kitchen, cooking equipment of the same size and description as in the Hall-place kitchen would have been used, but the superiority of the ingredients available here would have permitted much more interesting recipes. The following selection gives a good idea of the kind of dishes that would have been cooked here. The stocks of simple boiled meats, for example, could be converted into rather more luxurious pottages by the addition of beaten eggs stirred in just before serving.[25]

A POTTAGE CALLED GUSSET

1150ml (2pt) meat stock
50g (2oz) white breadcrumbs
2 large eggs, beaten
2.5ml ($\frac{1}{2}$ tsp) each of finely chopped thyme, savory, marjoram and parsley

1. Beat the herbs and breadcrumbs into the eggs, and add a little of the cold or warm stock.
2. Bring the rest of the stock almost to the boil, rapidly beat in the herbed breadcrumb mixture, and continue beating for a few minutes over a very gentle heat (it should not boil). Pour it into a deep dish, and serve.

The rather strange name of the next dish is derived from the Old English word 'sew', meaning a thick pottage or stew:

SHOES[26]

- 1350g (3lb) beef flank, skirt or brisket
- 1 large cabbage, coarsely sliced
- 1 pheasant or 2 partridges, drawn and trussed
- 5–10ml (1–2 tsp) salt

1. Half fill a large saucepan with water, bring it up to a rapid boil, put in the beef and lower the heat to a gentle simmer for 1½ hours.
2. Put in the birds and continue cooking for a further 30 minutes, then add the cabbage and simmer for 30 minutes more.
3. Add the salt to taste, stir, then lift the beef and birds out on to a large, deep dish, surround them with the cabbage, and fill the dish with the remaining stock just before serving.

For some boiled dishes, the meat was cooked quite plainly, the rich flavour coming from the 'sops', or pieces of bread, on which it was served.

SOPS FOR A CAPON[27]

- 1 chicken, drawn and trussed
- 225g (8oz) white bread
- 100g (4oz) butter
- 425ml (¾pt) claret
- 10ml (2 tsp) sugar
- 1.5ml (¼ tsp) ground ginger
- 1.5ml (¼ tsp) cinnamon
- 2 oranges, peeled and sliced

1. Simmer the chicken in water or light stock for 15–20 minutes per 450g (1lb), until tender.
2. Shortly before serving, mix the claret, sugar, spices and oranges in a saucepan, and cook them together for 5 minutes.
3. Slice the bread, cut it into large squares, shallow-fry it lightly in the butter, lay it in the bottom of a deep dish, and pour the claret sauce over it.
4. Drain the chicken, lay it on top, and serve.

CABBAGE[28]

1 large cabbage, quartered
1 large English onion, finely chopped
3 leeks, the whites finely chopped
1.5ml ($\frac{1}{4}$ tsp) ground cinnamon
pinch of saffron
1150–1725ml (2–3pt) light stock

1. *Simmer the vegetables and saffron in the stock for 20 minutes until just tender.*
2. *Place the vegetables in a large dish, pour in a little of the stock, and sprinkle with cinnamon. Serve immediately.*

CHARMERCHANDE[29]

450g (1lb) lean mutton or lamb
575ml (1pt) water
100g (4oz) fresh breadcrumbs
5ml (1 tsp) salt
5ml (1 tsp) chopped parsley
5ml (1 tsp) chopped sage

1. *Cube the meat, and simmer in the water for 1½–2 hours, until tender.*
2. *Stir in the remaining ingredients, stir until thickened, then serve.*

Around Christmas, the cooks would also boil large quantities of brawn in the Lord's-side kitchen for the upper household. The demand for this particular dish at this time of year was so great that at Greenwich Palace new ranges had to be built for the 'saything and boyling of brawnes'.[30] In the sixteenth century 'brawn' was not the jellied preparation of chopped pig's head and so on that we would recognise today, but a major joint of boar-meat. The forequarters, being the fattest, formed the 'brawn' for the upper households, and the remainder, called 'souse', went to the serving-men's tables. It was usually made of tame boar, since wild boar was already becoming extremely rare and would shortly become extinct in England. To ensure that the boars were in prime condition, they were usually penned up and specially fed from September.[31]

Put Boar in stye
Till Hallontide nigh.
With boar, good Ciss,
Let naught be amiss.

And then, in December:

Let boar life render,
See brawn sod [boiled] tender.

29. *The Lord's-side kitchen* Originally built for Cardinal Wolsey, this kitchen was later used to cook the meals served to the nobles and senior household officers who dined in the Council Chamber and Great Watching Chamber. It had its own boiling house (left) and doors leading left to the service road, forward into the Great Space, and right into the Scullery Yard.

The meat was rolled up and tied with bulrushes, osier or linen tape, and then plain-boiled until it was so soft that its fat could be pierced with a piece of straw or dry rush. It was lifted out and left to go cold, then put into barrels, which were filled up with either wine, ale or beer, plus cider vinegar and salt. Then it was stored in this way until required for use.

Today brawn is best cooked in spiced wine stock and consumed shortly afterwards:[32]

BRAWN

900 (2lb) rolled shoulder of pork
75cl (1 bottle) white wine
1 piece root ginger, chopped
45ml (3 tbs) salt
½ nutmeg, crushed
10ml (2 tsp) peppercorns
3 bay leaves

1. Put the wine, spices and bay leaves into a deep pan, add 575ml (1pt) water, and bring to the boil.
2. Put in the meat, skim it once it has returned to the boil, then simmer very gently for about 2 hours until tender.
3. Dissolve the salt in 1.7l (3pts) water. When the meat has cooked, put it into this cold brine and leave it in a cool place until it is to be served – within the next two or three days – then lift out, drain and slice.

Alternatively, use strong ale instead of the wine and spices, and proceed as above.

The stock left over after the meat has cooked may be made into a good pottage by stirring in 30ml (2 tbs) medium oatmeal, 5ml (1 tsp) dried sage or thyme, all mixed with a little cold water, and two coarsely sliced English onions. Simmer it for 40–45 minutes, then add salt and pepper to taste just before serving.

To serve the brawn in the sixteenth century, it was cut in slices and neatly arranged on a large dish. A stem of yew or gorse was dipped into egg white beaten to a froth or doused in water and sprinkled with flour, to resemble snow, and then stuck in the middle of the meat. Alternatively, a branch of gilded rosemary would be used. Small pieces of gold and silver leaf were then dotted on to the brawn, and three concentric rings of bay leaves stuck in vertically around its edge. A wide circle of red and yellow jelly was arranged just inside the well of the dish, and the rim then decorated with the same jellies, more brawn – sliced or stamped out with metal cutters – plus carved lemons, oranges, barberries, gilded bay leaves, beetroot, pickled barberries, gooseberries and grapes.[33]

The boar's head – the kind of brawn most celebrated of all at Christmas – was made by boning the head, stuffing it with a rich forcemeat, simmering it until it was cooked through, allowing it to cool, and then garnishing it in a similar manner to the dish just described.

It appeared as the first dish served on Christmas Day. In 1521 Wynkyn de Worde's *Christmasse Carolles* included one to accompany the bringing in of the boar's head:

The bore's head in hande bring I
With garlandes gay and rosemary.
I pray you all synge merely
Qui estis in convivio.

The bore's head, I understande,
Is the chefe servyce in this lande.
Loke wherever it be fande
Servite cum Cantico.

Be gladde, lords, both more and lasse,
For this hath ordayned our stewarde,
To chere you all this Christmasse,
The bores head with mustards!

Further details of how boars' heads were decorated in great houses at this period come from the household accounts of Hengrave Hall in Suffolk, where in December 1535 payments were made 'for 3 sheetes of thick grose paper to decke the bores heade in Christmas 12d. More payd to Bushe of Bury, paynter, for the paynting of the bores heade with sundry colors 12d'.[34]

The more routine Lord's-side dishes prepared at Hampton Court included not only the usual joints of beef, veal, mutton and lamb (roasted for approximately 20 minutes per pound (450g) plus 20 minutes, given a good fire), but also a much more varied range of poultry and game. The birds were plucked and drawn – any trussing done with linen tape, skewers and bodkins – then prepared as follows:[35]

Heron	The wings cut off, the legs folded up, the bone removed from the neck; then the bird would be mounted on the spit, the neck wound around it and secured by sticking the bill into the breast.
Bittern	As above, but leaving the wings on.
Curlew	As for the heron, but removing the lower bill and sticking the upper bill into the shoulder.
Woodcock	The wings cut off, the legs folded up, and the bill put through both thighs.
Snipe	As for the woodcock, but with the bill through the shoulder.
Plover	The lower part of the legs cut off, and also the wings.

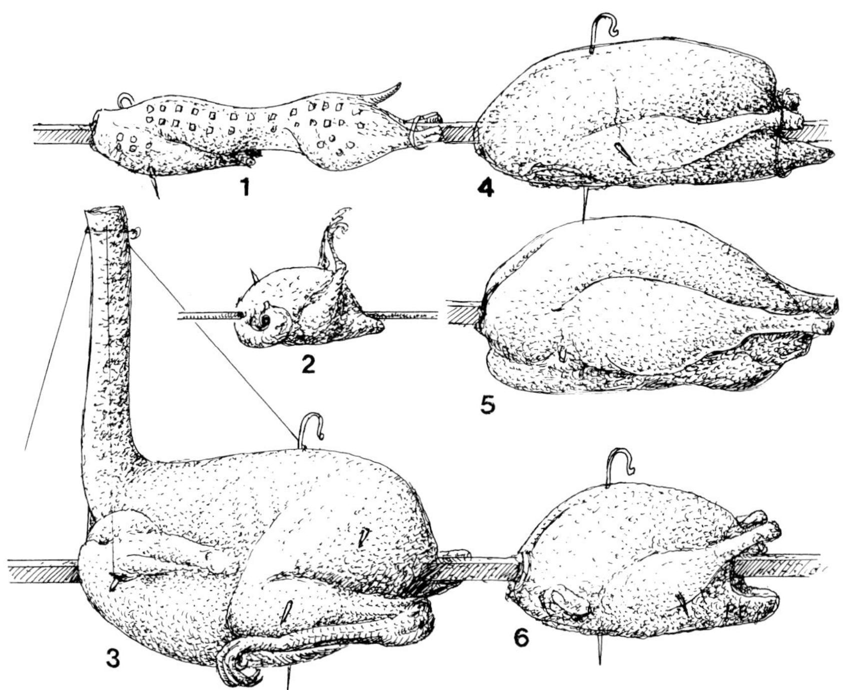

30. *Trussing* Tudor recipe books give detailed instructions for trussing meat for the spit: rabbits were parboiled and larded (1); snipe had their bills stuck through their shoulders (2); peacocks had their legs folded and necks set erect (3); and ducks, geese and chickens had their wings and lower legs removed (4–6).

Chicken	The head removed, the feet left on. If to be 'endored', it was basted with a batter made of egg yolk, flour, ginger, pepper, saffron and salt.
Rabbit	Parboiled, then larded with narrow strips of fat bacon.

The fish cooked in the Lord's-side kitchen was simmered and broiled as in the Hall-place kitchen, but, as Alexander Barclay enviously noted, fish for the more important members of the court was also:

Roasted or sodden in sweet herbs or wine,
Or fried in oil most saperous and fine.

TO FRY WHITINGS[36]

700g (1lb 8oz) whiting or other white fish
100g (4oz) butter or 100ml (4fl oz) oil
15ml (1 tbs) wine vinegar
1.5ml (¼ tsp) mace
1.5 ml (¼ tsp) pepper

225g (8 oz) apples or onions, finely chopped
275ml (½pt) white wine
pinch of ground cloves
5ml (1 tsp) salt
a little flour

1. Fry the apples or onions in a little of the butter or oil in a saucepan until cooked but not browned. Stir in the wine, vinegar, salt, pepper and spices, cook for a few minutes more, and keep hot ready for use.
2. Skin the filleted fish, dust with flour, fry in the remaining butter or oil for 5–10 minutes. Serve with the sauce.

Fritters were also part of the Lord's-side repertoire:

APPLE FRITTERS[37]

3 or 4 cooking apples
100g (4oz) plain flour
175ml (6fl oz) ale
sugar for sprinkling
pinch of saffron
1.5ml (¼ tsp) salt
oil for frying

1. Mix the flour, saffron and salt in a bowl. Make a well in the centre and pour in the ale little by little, while beating, to form a smooth, thick coating batter, adding a little more ale or water if needed.
2. Peel and core the apples, and cut them across into medium slices.
3. Heat oil in a deep chip pan, or pour 1.3cm (½in) oil into a frying pan, and heat until it will cook a little batter dropped into it. Then dip each apple slice in turn into the batter on both sides, shake off any surplus, and put it into the hot fat, turning it to cook on both sides until puffed up and pale brown. Then remove with a skimmer and place on a hot dish, repeating this with the other slices.
4. Sprinkle with sugar just before serving.

SPINACH FRITTERS[38]

225g (8oz) cooked and drained spinach
50g (2oz) fresh white breadcrumbs
2 eggs beaten
1.5ml (¼ tsp) cinnamon
1.5ml (¼ tsp) ginger
50g (2oz) or more butter
sugar for sprinkling

1. Chop or blend the spinach, breadcrumbs and spices, and beat in enough egg to form a soft paste.
2. Heat a little butter in a frying pan, drop in a tablespoon of the

31. *The kitchen chimneys* The north wall of the kitchens, facing on to Tennis Court Lane, is a magnificent example of early-sixteenth-century brickwork. The wide doorway provides the only access into the kitchens from the north, and was essential for bringing in the tons of logs required to keep the ten great fireplaces constantly ablaze in the kitchens and workhouses.

paste, spreading and levelling it with the back of a spoon and shaking the pan to ensure that it does not stick. Then fry on both sides and remove to a hot dish, continuing until all the mixture has been used.
3. Serve sprinkled with sugar on a hot dish.

Although salad ingredients do not occur in the royal ordinances and dietaries – probably because they were grown in-house and so did not need to be purchased and financially accounted for – they do appear on menus and in other sources from this period. They usually carry a health warning, such as 'beware of saledis, grene metis, & frutes rawe, for they make many a man have a feble mawe', or 'beware of grene sallettes & rawe fruytes, for they wyll make your sovrayne seke [sick]'.[39] All the same, there had been a long tradition of eating salads in England. One royal recipe of 1393 included parsley, sage, garlic, spring onions, leek, borage, mint, fennel, garden cress, rue, rosemary and purslane, to be washed, picked clean, mixed with olive oil and sprinkled with vinegar and salt. In the sixteenth century similar salads were being made in an almost identical way, except that lettuces were included and the salt was replaced with sugar. Simple salads now contained lettuce dressed with oil, vinegar and sugar, or cold boiled onions, asparagus or samphire, or cucumbers dressed with oil, vinegar and pepper. However, other salads were much more complex:[40]

SALLAD FOR GREAT FEASTS AND PRINCES' TABLES

- 50g (2oz) each of sliced, blanched almonds, raisins, thinly sliced figs and capers
- 225g (8oz) olives
- 100g (4oz) currants
- 50g (2oz) sugar
- 90ml (6 tbs) olive oil
- 30ml (2 tbs) wine vinegar
- 2 oranges, peeled and sliced crossways
- 2 lemons, peeled and sliced crossways
- a few sage leaves
- 100g (4oz) raw spinach leaves
- 1 lettuce heart, sliced crossways
- inner leaves of a red cabbage (as substitute for red cauliflower leaves)
- ½ cucumber, sliced and soaked in vinegar

1. Mix together the almonds, dried fruits, capers, spinach and half the olives, dress them with the oil, vinegar and sugar in a deep dish.
2. Cover the mixture with half the orange and lemon slices arranged in circles, put a thin layer of red cabbage leaves on top, then the remaining olives, the cucumber slices and the lettuce, all arranged in circles. Decorate the rim with the rest of the orange and lemon slices.

The meals would have been served from the dresser hatches into the Great Space, where waiters would carry them a few paces to the dresser office for checking by the clerks, before taking them up to the Great Watching Chamber. Dishes such as these, along with the rich meat pies and fruit tarts from the Bakehouse, would have provided the senior courtiers and senior household staff with excellent fare.

✿

At the east side of the Great Space, next door to the Lord's-side kitchen-workhouse, were two rooms (no. 46) used as lodgings by the clerk of the kitchen, a spiral staircase in one corner leading up to the first-floor chambers (no. 47). These rooms were occupied by the Queen's groom porter, the officers of the Wafery, and the master surgeon and yeoman surgeon, together with their groom and either a servant or an 'honest child'.[41] While it was the doctor of physic who advised on the King's diet, concocted his medicines and sought out lepers and those with contagious diseases at court, the surgeons were responsible for all the more practical aspects of health care.[42] As well as carrying out actual surgery, they received an allowance of 'broken meats' left over after meals, which presumably included fats for ointments, bread for poultices and so on. Worn-out cloths and towels from the Ewery they used to make bandages and plasters for sick officers of the court. Some of these items, together with medicines for the King's use, were stored in these chambers in a small coffer.

Details of the organisation of a surgical operation at court, and the roles played by the kitchen staff, appear in an account of the trial of Sir Edmund Knevet, held at Greenwich on 10 June 1541.[43] Having been found guilty of striking one Master Clere at the King's court, Sir Edmund was sentenced to lose his right hand, and so the appropriate officers were assembled. The yeoman of the scullery brought two forms to hold the equipment: the sergeant of the woodyard brought his mallet and chopping block, the King's master cook brought his knife – and the sergeant of the poultry brought a cock which would have its head cut off with these items so as to check that they were in good order. The sergeant of the larder, with his great knowledge of butchery, was there to set the knife in the best position on the wrist, and the sergeant farrier brought his searing irons – for sealing the veins – these first being heated in a chafing dish and their ends cooled in a dish of water brought by the yeoman of the scullery. The sergeant surgeon was in attendance with his instruments to close up the wound, which would then be dressed with 'sear-cloth' brought by the yeoman of the chandlery. In addition, the sergeant of the cellar brought wine, ale and beer, and the yeoman of the ewery, deputising for his sergeant, brought a ewer, a basin and towels for hand-washing.

Fortunately, Sir Edmund's appeal to the King was successful, and he both kept his hand and received a full pardon. But this description clearly shows how closely the surgeons and the household staff were expected to work together, and suggests how useful they would all be when on active military service.

The last room in this first-floor area that should be mentioned is the Wafery. This office produced wafers – broad discs or rectangles of thin, crisp,

32. *Wafers* Here iron wafer-tongs cut with the Tudor royal arms are being filled with an egg, flour, sugar and rosewater batter before being cooked over the chafing dish.

delicately-flavoured biscuit, made only for the King, dukes, earls, the White Sticks, the cofferer, and a privileged few as authorised by the Counting House. Lesser mortals might only enjoy them at the four great feasts of the year.[44] The yeoman of the wafery, assisted by a groom skilled in wafer-making and, at the discretion of the Counting House, a page to learn the craft and give general assistance, were solely responsible to the clerk of the spicery. The sugar, eggs and baking irons they needed came from the Spicery, while the flour was obtained from the sergeant of the bakehouse either daily or weekly. A sweet spiced batter would be made, then small quantities ladled on to the 'irons' – flat plates engraved with various patterns and mounted on long handles like tongs – which had been pre-heated over a charcoal-fired chafing dish.

Wafers may be made in the same way today, using one of the early recipes and one of the iron or aluminium wafer-irons still available in Belgium and Holland.

TO MAKE WAFERS[45]

225g (8oz) plain flour
1.5ml ($\frac{1}{4}$ tsp) cinnamon
30ml (2 tbs) sugar
2 egg yolks

150ml ($\frac{1}{4}$pt) cream
30ml (2 tbs) rosewater
25g (1oz) butter

1. Mix the flour, cinnamon and sugar in a bowl, and make a well in the centre. Pour in the eggs and rosewater and beat them in, adding the cream little by little, with some water if necessary to form a stiff batter (rather thicker than that used for pancakes).
2. Heat the closed irons on one side and then on the other over a stove. Wrap the butter in a small piece of cloth, and use it to very lightly grease the inside faces of the irons.
3. Pour a small pool of batter into the middle of the inside face of one iron, then quickly close the irons and keep them pressed firmly together as the wafer cooks – sending out plumes of steam and squeaks, whines and squeals as it does so!
4. When the steam starts to subside and before you smell scorching, open the irons and remove the wafer – either flat, to dry off on a cooling rack, or rolled off on the handle of a wooden spoon and left to dry.

The wafers should be crisp and light-coloured, but this requires skill in mixing the batter and judging the temperature, which will take some time to acquire.

The newly baked wafers would be carefully locked away in fine coffers. When the time came, they would be delivered to the sewer of the privy chamber, for the King's mouth; to the sewers of the presence chamber, for distribution as directed by the Counting House; or to the sewer of the hall – to be served there only on the important feast days.

8

The Privy Kitchen

Food for the King

The hall-place and Lord's-side kitchens were designed to serve the household servants and the courtiers with their main meals at ten and four o'clock each day, the vast scale of their operations making any unexpected changes in their routines extremely difficult to manage. It would therefore have been impossible for them also to meet the needs of a monarch, especially one as mobile as Henry VIII, who was usually unwilling to return to the palace 'upon the time prefixed for dinner and souper', particularly if he had 'gone further in walkeing, hunting, hawking, or other disports'.[1] These activities made it essential for him to be served by a separate office, the Privy Kitchen. Flexibility of mealtimes was only one of the advantages of this arrangement; perhaps more importantly, it also protected him from the risk of poisoning, ensured the security of the rarest and most expensive of foodstuffs in the kitchen, and enabled the King's personal cooks to create the finest of dishes in kitchens that were entirely under their own control. In addition, special diets could be prepared for the King and the closest members of the royal family, as advised by the physician.

In the 1540s the King's privy kitchen was located beneath his Long Gallery in the wing separating the present Clock Court and Fountain Court; the Queen's privy kitchen, built in 1533 for Anne Boleyn, was beneath her Presence Chamber, midway between the chapel and Fountain Court.[2] In these positions the two kitchens were ideally situated to provide hot food directly to the rooms in which the King and the Queen took their meals, as well as keeping their personal apartments extra-warm and comfortable. Working from the dietaries of the King and Queen, and the recipes which probably derive from the Privy Kitchen (some of which were published in the second half of the sixteenth century), it is possible to make informed suggestions as to the dishes prepared here by Pero, the French cook to the King's mouth, and his fellows.

TO BOIL A LEG OF MUTTON[3]

900g (2lb) leg of lamb or mutton
1150ml (2pt) lamb stock
575ml (1pt) white wine
150ml (¼pt) wine vinegar
1 lemon, thinly sliced
zest of half an orange peel, finely shredded
15ml (1 tbs) sugar
1.5ml (¼ tsp) cinnamon
1.5ml (¼ tsp) ginger
25g (1oz) fresh white breadcrumbs
225g (8oz) 2.5cm (1in) cubed white bread
1.5ml (¼ tsp) salt

1. *Pre-heat the oven to 180°C (350°F, gas mark 4).*
2. *Put the meat in a roasting tin and bake for 15 minutes. Remove it from the oven, put a metal plate on top, press it down as hard as possible, then slash the meat with a knife and press again. Pour the juices into a small saucepan.*
3. *Return the meat to the oven again for 10 minutes, then repeat the pressing. Put it back in the oven for 10 minutes more, and press again. By now you should have about 45ml (3 tbs) of juice.*
4. *Mix the lamb stock, wine and vinegar in a large saucepan, and bring to the boil. Put in the par-roast meat, reduce to a simmer, and continue cooking for 45–50 minutes until tender.*
5. *When the meat is ready, add the salt, lemon slices, orange zest, sugar, spices and breadcrumbs to the small saucepan containing the meat juices, then ladle in 425ml (¾pt) of stock from the simmering lamb and cook for 5 minutes.*
6. *Line the bottom of a deep dish with the cubed bread, put the meat on top, pour the sauce over it, arrange the lemon slices on the joint, and garnish around the rim with a little sugar.*

WHITE BROTH WITH ALMONDS[4]

900g (2lb) leg of lamb, cubed
1.1l (2pt) light stock
2.5ml (½ tsp) salt
25g (1oz) butter
blade of mace
15ml (1 tbs) cider vinegar
small bouquet of rosemary, thyme, hyssop and marjoram
225g (8oz) 2.5cm (1in) cubed white bread
50g (2oz) ground almonds
20ml (4 tsp) sugar
2.5ml (½ tsp) ground ginger
15ml (1 tbs) rosewater
1 orange, thinly sliced

1. Gently simmer the lamb, salt, butter, mace, vinegar and bouquet with the stock, adding just enough water to cover it, for 2½–3 hours, until tender.
2. Beat the almonds in a mortar with a little of the stock from the pot, strain the liquid through a cloth into a small saucepan, add the ginger, rosewater and half the sugar, and give it a quick boil.
3. In another pan, simmer the orange slices and remaining sugar with a little stock from the pot.
4. When the lamb is ready, arrange the bread in the bottom of a deep dish, pour the stew on top of it, then the almond sauce – and finally the oranges, just before serving.

LEG OF MUTTON WITH LEMONS[5]

900g (2lb) leg of lamb, cubed
30ml (2 tbs) sugar
225g (8oz) 2.5cm (1in cubes of white bread
75g (3oz) currants
15ml (1 tbs) cider vinegar
1.5ml (¼ tsp) ground pepper
a few drops of red food colouring

1. Put the meat in a saucepan with just enough water to cover it, and stew for 2 hours. Then add the remaining ingredients except the bread and continue cooking for about another 45 minutes until tender.
2. Arrange the bread in the bottom of a deep dish, and pour the lamb on top just before serving.

By remarkable good fortune, one manuscript cookery book (later owned by Samuel Pepys) has a whole section of recipes for 'Gentyll manly Cokere and copyd of the sergent to the kyng', which give precise instruction on how the food was cooked, presumably by a Tudor sergeant cook for the King's mouth, in the privy kitchen.[6] They are of the highest quality, as may be seen in the following examples prefixed 'Sergeant of the King's . . .'

SERGEANT OF THE KING'S CAPONS STEWED[7]

one 2.7kg (6lb) chicken
large quantity of fresh parsley, sage, rosemary and thyme
37cl (½ bottle) red wine
30ml (2 tbs) sugar
1.5ml (¼ tsp) salt
1.5ml (¼ tsp) ground cinnamon
75cl (1 bottle) white wine
50g (2oz) chopped dates
25g (1oz) currants
1.5ml (¼ tsp) ground ginger
225g (8oz) 2.5cm (1in) cubed white bread

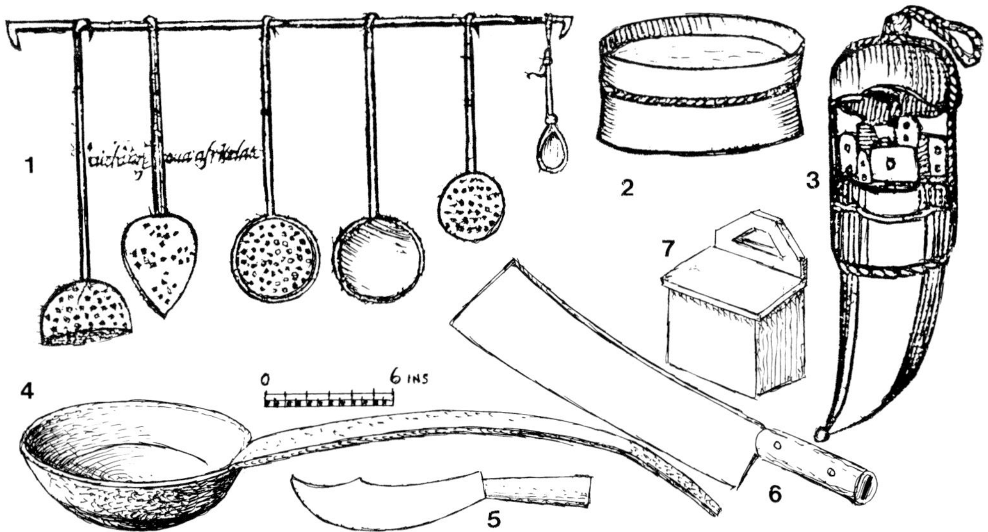

33. *Kitchen equipment* This selection shows skimmers on their rack (1), a hair sieve (2), and a sheath of cook's knives (3) as illustrated by Scappi in 1570. The frying pan (4) was used in Norwich in 1507, the knife (5) in Bristol in 1479, and the cleaver (6) at Northcott Manor, Middlesex, in the early fifteenth century; the salt-box (7) is based on a carving of c.1500 in Manchester Cathedral.

1. Stuff the chicken with half the herbs. Put the remainder, with the chicken, into a large pan, using a grid or a couple of spoons to prevent it sitting on the bottom. Cover with water, bring to the boil, skim, and reduce to a gentle simmer for 2 hours.
2. 10 minutes before serving, heat together the remaining ingredients except the bread to make a sauce.
3. Arrange the bread in a deep dish, place the drained chicken on top, and pour the sauce over it just before serving.

The term 'in douce' usually indicated that the food was sweetened with sugar, as in the following recipe:

SERGEANT OF THE KING'S CAPONS IN DOUCE[8]

1 chicken
100g (4oz) ground almonds
225g (8oz) white bread cut in 2.5cm (1in) cubes, and toasted golden-brown
2.5ml (½ tsp) salt
275ml (½ pt) white wine
pinch of saffron
30ml (2 tbs) sugar
butter or oil for roasting

1. Roast the chicken with a little butter or oil at 200°C (400°F, gas mark 6) allowing 20 minutes per 450g (1lb) plus 20 minutes.
2. Soak the almonds in water for 30 minutes, drain, then grind with 575ml (1pt) water, adding and pouring it off little by little and straining it through a cloth to make almond milk.
3. Put the almond milk into a small saucepan, add the saffron, sugar and salt, bring to the boil, stir in half the wine, and set to one side.
4. Arrange the toasted bread in a deep dish, pour the rest of the wine over it, leave it for 5 minutes, then pour on the almond milk sauce and place the roast chicken on top just before serving.

SERGEANT OF THE KING'S MEAT STEW[9]

1350g (3lb) lean steak
1150ml (2pt) red wine
450g (1lb) English onions, sliced
30ml (2 tbs) honey
100g (4oz) raisins
50g (2oz) ground almonds, bruised
1.5ml (¼ tsp) each of ground cloves, pepper, ginger and mace
pinch of saffron
2.5ml (½ tsp) each of chopped sage, rosemary, thyme and hyssop
225g (8oz) white bread cut into 2.5cm (1in) cubes

1. Place all the ingredients, except the bread, into a pan and simmer for 2½–3 hours, stirring very occasionally. Arrange the bread on the bottom of a deep dish, and pour the stew on top just before serving.

BOILED ONIONS[10]

450g (1lb) English onions
75g (3oz) raisins
5ml (1 tsp) ground pepper
225g (8oz) white bread cut into 2.5cm (1in) cubes
2.5ml (½ tsp) salt
275ml (½ pt) water
1 egg yolk
15ml (1 tbs) vinegar
15ml (1 tbs) sugar

1. Peel and quarter the onions, and simmer with the raisins, pepper, salt and water for 15 minutes. Put the bread in a deep dish.
2. Beat the egg yolk and vinegar together, and stir into the onion mixture just before pouring it over the cubed bread.

The roasts prepared for the King were similarly rich and flavoursome. The first recipe (below) is of particular interest, since it records how a fresh-killed chicken had a cut made in the back of its neck into which the cook blew hard, inflating the skin like a balloon and separating it from the flesh.

Once the chicken had been drawn, washed and had its head removed, the space between the skin and the flesh was packed with a rich stuffing, which was first set in place by parboiling. Then the chicken was lifted from the pot and spit-roasted before the fire. As it rotated, the fats and flavours of the stuffing permeated the chicken, while its juices were encased inside the stuffing layer. The result was the most succulent and delicious of dishes.

At a Hampton Court kitchen demonstration two of the visitors were very surprised to see chickens being cooked in this way. It turned out that the method was identical to one that they regularly used at home in Malta. It was fascinating to discover that this recipe, brought to England from the Mediterranean by returning Crusaders some eight hundred years ago, along with so many other fine Arab dishes, was still flourishing today in one of its countries of origin.

SERGEANT OF THE KING'S CHICKENS FARCED[11]

1 large oven-ready chicken
3 hard-boiled egg yolks
1 large egg, beaten
25g (1oz) currants
1 small tin chopped pork
5ml (1 tsp) each of parsley, sage and thyme

1. *Scald the herbs, drain immediately, and leave to cool.*
2. *Create a space between the body and the skin of the chicken by inserting the fingers from both ends.*
3. *Mix the egg yolks, raw egg, currants, pork and herbs together to form a smooth forcemeat, and pack this evenly between the skin and the flesh. Then truss the chicken for roasting.*
4. *Pre-heat the oven to 200°C (400°F, gas mark 6). Plunge the chicken into a large pan of boiling water for 15 minutes, then remove. Place immediately on a grid in a roasting tin, and roast for 20 minutes per 450g (1lb) uncooked chicken, plus 20 minutes.*
5. *The chicken may be dredged with flour and basted with butter about 30 minutes after it has been put in the oven.*

In the following recipe, thin slices of steak are rolled and stuffed to resemble larks, taking their name from *aloe*, the Old French word for this small bird. Today this dish is better known as 'beef olives'.

SERGEANT OF THE KING'S ALLOES OF BEEF (beef olives)[12]

6 large, thin frying steaks
5ml (1 tsp) thyme, chopped
5ml (1 tsp) sage, chopped
75g (3oz) suet

34. *Graffiti* This stag was probably scratched into the masonry at the side of the Hall-place dresser by a Tudor or Stuart cook, and represents the royal venison cooked across in the Privy Kitchen but never officially tasted here.

- 1 large English onion, finely chopped
- salt and pepper

1. Lightly beat the steaks, and sprinkle with salt and pepper.
2. Mix together the onion, herbs and suet, spread this over the steaks, roll them up, then tie them securely with thin string.
3. For spit-roasting, the strings at the ends of the rolls may be tied to the spits. For oven baking, each roll can be threaded on to a skewer supported across a baking tin, and cooked at 170°C (325°F, gas mark 3) for about 40 minutes. Then cut off the strings and serve.

The dietaries restricted the serving of venison to the tables of the King and Queen. Andrew Boorde held this meat in the highest esteem:

> I am sure it is a lordes disshe, and I am sure it is good for an Englisshe man, for it doth anymate hym to be as he is, whiche is stronge and hardy, but I do advertyse every man, for all my wordes, not to kyll, and so to eate of it, excepte it be [lawfully], for it is a meate for great

men. And great men do not set so much by the meate, as they do by the pastyme of kyllyng of it . . . there is not so moche pleasure for harte & hynde, bucke, and doo, and for roo bucke and doo, as here in Englande.[13]

SERGEANT OF THE KING'S SIDES OF FAT DEER ROASTED[14]

1 joint of venison
575ml (1pt) red wine
5ml (1 tsp) salt
2.5ml (½ tsp) ground black pepper

1. Weigh the joint, and calculate the roasting time at 30 minutes per 450g (1lb). Spit it, and continually turn and baste it with the wine, salt and black pepper. Or place it on a grid in a roasting tin, then in an oven pre-heated to 170°C (325°F, gas mark 3), with the wine etc. and baste it regularly.
2. When cooked, place the venison on a hot dish and pour the liquor from the pan over it just before serving.

For centuries, the accompaniment to roast venison was frumenty – a sort of whole-wheat porridge which Boorde commended, for, 'when it is digested it doth nourysshe, and it doth strength a man'.[15]

FRUMENTY

175g (6oz) whole wheat
100g (4oz) ground almonds
2 raw egg yolks
large pinch of saffron
275ml (½ pt) light stock

1. Bruise the wheat in a pestle and mortar, then put it into a pan, scald it with hot water, and leave it in a cool place to soak for 1–2 days.
2. Add more water to the wheat, so that the pan contains three times its volume of water, and leave in a warm oven or on a very gentle heat for at least a day to swell and cook. Then leave it to cool overnight.
3. Blend the almonds with the stock and strain it to make almond milk. Beat it with the egg yolks and saffron, and then beat this into the wheat.
4. Heat the wheat almost to boiling, and serve in a deep dish. If you are using pearl barley as a substitute for wheat, you need to simmer it in water for only about 45 minutes before proceeding from stage 3.

A similar alternative could also be made with rice:[16]

RICE OF GENOA

100g (4oz) rice
1.7l (3pt) stock
5ml (1 tsp) salt
large pinch of saffron

Bring the stock to the boil, stir in the remaining ingredients, and simmer for 20 minutes, stirring to prevent it from sticking and burning.

Another roast suitable for the royal table was peacock. Various authors have given peacock a poor reputation, describing it as tough and unpleasant. This may originate in historical references such as this comment in Andrewe's *Noble Lyfe*: 'it is evyll flesshe to disiest [digest], for it can nat be rosted or soden ynough', while Andrew Boorde confirmed that 'olde pecockes be harde of dygestyon [but] young peachycken of halfe a yere of age by praysed'.[17] The royal cooks certainly appreciated this difference when making their peacock 'in hakille ryally' ('hackle' being the medieval word for a bird's skin and plumage), or for 'a Feesste Roiall', for which the peacock had its unplucked skin put back in place after being roasted.[18] Whenever this dish is depicted complete with its tail feathers, they are seen to be those of a young, tender bird, not the fully developed ones of an old one.[19] Certainly, modern farmed peacocks eat very well – they have a flavour midway between chicken and pheasant, and large breasts and legs ideal for carving.

PEACOCK ROYAL[20]

1 peacock, undrawn, unplucked
3–4 egg yolks, beaten
ground cumin
1 piece of gold leaf

1. *Lay the peacock on its back, cut round the skin at the top of each leg, then make another cut from the top of one leg across to the top of the other. From this point remove the skin from the lower part of the bird, cutting off the root of the tail internally, to keep it intact. Then remove the skin from the upper part of the bird, cutting off the last joint of the wings internally. Finally, peel the skin from the neck by pulling it inside out towards the head, up to the topmost vertebra, cutting through the neck at this point.*
2. *Turn the skin completely inside out and thickly dust the flesh side with the cumin.*
3. *Draw the peacock, truss the legs close to the body as if it were sitting on a perch, and insert a long skewer down the full length of the neck. Slide the peacock on to a spit, and use string or thin wire to truss the neck in an upright position (see p. 135). Brush with the egg yolks*

and roast for 20 minutes per 450g (1lb) plus 20 minutes. Alternatively, place the trussed peacock on a grid in a roasting tin and cook at 200°C (400°F, gas mark 6) for the same time.

The recipes then state that the peacock should be allowed to cool a little, which allows the neck to set in position, then its skin is replaced and its beak gilded with the gold leaf, just before serving. Today it is preferable to mount the skin on a chicken-wire frame to appear as if complete. You present this to the table, then return it to the kitchen, from where you now serve the real peacock without any risk of contamination from the raw skin. Traditionally, the peacock was accompanied by finely ground ginger or sauce ginger.

In addition to being roasted and boiled, white meats were also served as a 'mortis' or 'blancmange', a sort of sweet pâté thickened with rice flour, breadcrumbs or almonds.[21]

TO MAKE A MORTIS

half a chicken
50g (2oz) ground almonds
150ml (¼pt) milk
15ml (1 tbs) sugar
15ml (1 tbs) rosewater

1. *Put the chicken into a saucepan, cover it with water, and simmer until tender, about 45 minutes. Now blend the almonds with the milk to form a smooth cream.*
2. *Drain the chicken, pick off the flesh, chop it, then blend it with the almond cream and the sugar. Place it in a saucepan and cook over a gentle heat for 10–15 minutes, stirring continuously as it thickens.*
3. *Cool the saucepan in a bowl of cold water, beat in the rosewater, then fork the resulting pâté into a deep bowl or make a round shape on a plate. Serve it when entirely cold.*

As for fish, although the King and Queen enjoyed a much greater choice of species, the methods of cookery would have been very similar to those used in the hall-place and Lord's-side kitchens. They would also have enjoyed superior dishes such as these two:[22]

SERGEANT OF THE KING'S MORTRESS OF FISH

450g (1lb) haddock or cod
75g (3oz) ground almonds
15ml (1 tbs) sugar
15ml (1 tbs) icing sugar

175g (6oz) fresh white breadcrumbs
5ml (1 tsp) ground ginger

1. *Put the fish in a shallow pan, just cover with water, and simmer for about 10 minutes, until tender.*
2. *Lift the fish on to a plate and remove all the skin and bones.*
3. *Blend the almonds with 425ml (¾pt) of the fish stock from the pan (together with the cooked liver of the fish, if available), then blend in the fish, breadcrumbs and sugar.*
4. *Pour the mixture into a pan and cook for a few minutes, stirring continuously until it has thickened. Then pour it into serving dishes, leave it to cool, and sprinkle with the mixed ginger and icing sugar just before serving.*

SERGEANT OF THE KING'S SALMON ROASTED IN SAUCE[23]

6 salmon steaks
1 large or 2 small English onions
575ml (1pt) red wine
2.5ml (½ tsp) ground cinnamon
15ml (1 tbs) wine vinegar
5ml (1 tsp) salt
5 ml (1 tsp) ground ginger

1. *Finely chop the onion, place in a saucepan with the wine and cinnamon, cover, and cook for 15 minutes.*
2. *Place the salmon on a grid and cook over charcoal or beneath a gas or electric grill for 4–7 minutes each side, depending on the thickness of the steaks.*
3. *When the onions and salmon are both cooked, place the salmon on a hot dish. Then stir the vinegar, ginger and salt into the onions, and pour this sauce over the salmon just before serving.*

The King was also served with puddings, these being largely meat or cereal mixtures cooked in skins, just like the black puddings, hog's puddings and haggises which still survive from medieval times. Probably because she had a good reputation for her puddings, 'the wif that makes the king podinges at hamptoncourte' was paid 6s 8d from the Privy Purse expenses.[24] She probably worked outside the royal household, bringing in her wares as required.

WHITE PUDDINGS OF HOG'S LIVER[25]

375g (1lb 5oz) pig's liver
275ml (½pt) cream
2.5ml (½ tsp) mixed ground cloves, mace and saffron

6 egg yolks and 2 of the whites
225g (8oz) suet
50g (2oz) chopped dates
50g (2oz) raisins
225g (8oz) fresh white bread-crumbs
15ml (1 tbs) sugar
sausage skins

1. Parboil the liver, pound smooth in a mortar or food-processor, then stir in the remaining ingredients.
2. Pack the mixture into the skins using a funnel, tie up the ends, and plunge the puddings into a large pot of boiling salted water, then simmer them for 30 minutes.
3. Either serve hot, or store in a cool place for no more than two days, then eat them cold or fry until lightly browned.

The King's and Queen's dietaries included a number of sweet dishes such as custards, fritters, 'dowcets', tarts, 'rascals', jelly and cream of almonds, all made in the privy kitchen. These dishes, in addition to the fruit – baked pippins, oranges, quinces and so on – provided by the Confectionary, featured in their everyday meals as well as being served at 'banquets', those most exclusive of informal entertainments at which sweetmeats and fine wines were served, either in privy chambers or in the banqueting houses which stood in the Privy Gardens to the south of the palace. Some of these dishes were quite plain: 'rascals', alias 'resquyles', or 'rysmole' simply being a ground-rice cream:[26]

RYSMOLE

50g (2oz) rice flour
50g (2oz) ground almonds
small pinch of salt
45ml (3 tbs) sugar
2.5ml (½ tsp) ground ginger

1. Blend the almonds with 275ml (½pt) water. Add the rice flour, blend again, and put the mixture into a pan with a further 275ml (½pt) water, and the remaining ingredients.
2. Cook gently, stirring continuously, until the mixture has thickened and boiled. Then pour into a dish and serve either hot or cold.

Almond cream was similarly bland, but being 'made with fyne sugar and good rose-water and eaten with the flowers of many vyolettes, is a commendable dysshe, specyallye in Lent, it comfortes the brayne, & doth qualyfye the heate of the lyvver':[27]

SERGEANT OF THE KING'S CREAM OF ALMONDS

100g (4oz) ground almonds
575ml (1pt) water
15ml (1 tbs) white wine vinegar
60ml (4 tbs) white wine or rosewater
30ml (2 tbs) sugar

1. *Blend the almonds with half the water until very smooth. Strain the liquid into a saucepan, blend the residue with the remaining water, and strain it into the pan once more.*
2. *Heat the almond milk to the boil while stirring, pour in the vinegar, remove from the heat, and leave to stand for 10 minutes.*
3. *Place a double layer of muslin across a bowl, pour in the curdled almond milk and hang it up to drain, squeezing gently to remove the surplus liquid.*
4. *Turn the almond curd into a bowl, stir in the wine or rosewater and sugar, pour into a bowl, and serve with wafers.*

In contrast, jellies had been among the most spectacular dishes to be made in the royal kitchens for centuries. At the coronation of Henry VI in 1429, for example, there had been 'Gely party wryten and noted [inscribed] with "Te Deum laudamus"' and 'A white leche (see p. 155) wyth a red antelop, with a crowne about his necke with a chayne of golde'.[28] Francesco Chiergató, the apostolic nuncio in England, had marvelled at the jellies that Henry VIII had served to the Spanish embassy in 1517 – 'but the jellies of some 20 sorts perhaps, surpassed everything, they were made in the shape of castles and animals of various descriptions, as beautiful and admirable as can be imagined'.[29] The original recipes call for calves' feet and similar gelatinous materials to be boiled, strained and clarified – time-consuming processes that made jellies very expensive to produce – but today they can be made with ready-prepared gelatin to produce identical results. The jelly listed in the Henrician dietary was called 'jelly ipocras', since it was essentially a jellified form of the sweet spiced wine of that name:[30]

JELLY HIPPOCRAS

275ml (½pt) claret
100g (4oz) sugar
2–3 pieces root ginger
5cm (2in) stick cinnamon
¼ whole nutmeg
6 cloves
a few coriander seeds
pinch of salt
20ml (4 tsp) gelatin

1. Lightly bruise the spices and gently simmer with the salt and 275ml (½pt) water for 10 minutes.
2. Pour half the claret into a jug, stir in the sugar and gelatin, then strain in the hot spiced liquid through a paper coffee-filter. Stir until the gelatin has dissolved, stir in the remaining claret, pour into a serving dish, and leave to set.

Its flavour contrasted admirably with the other main variety of jelly, the 'leach'. This word, which simply means 'slice', was used to describe a luscious, cool, perfumed mass of translucent whiteness, solid enough to be cut into cubes and lifted to the lips with the fingers:[31]

WHITE LEACH

575ml (1pt) milk	100g (4oz) sugar
20ml (4 tsp) gelatin	25ml (1½ tbs) rosewater

1. Heat the milk to around 60°C (140°F), sprinkle in the gelatin, stir until dissolved, then stir in the sugar and rosewater. Pour into a lightly greased, shallow rectangular metal or plastic tray.
2. When set, turn it out on to a freshly rinsed cloth, cut into cubes with a wet knife, and arrange on a serving dish.

As well as making these and many other 'banqueting stuffs', the Privy Kitchen would prepare various hot nightcaps for the royal family. One of these was 'aleberry', which was served in the special aleberry bowl listed in the inventory of 1547:[32]

ALEBERRY

575ml (1pt) strong brown ale	1.5ml (¼ tsp) ground cloves
45g (3 tbs) fine oatmeal	1.5ml (¼ tsp) ground mace
45ml (3 tbs) sugar	225g (8oz) crustless white bread cut in 2.5cm (1in) cubes

1. Mix the oatmeal, spices and sugar in a pan with a little of the ale, then add the remaining ale. Bring to the boil, and simmer while stirring for a further 10–15 minutes, until thick and smooth.
2. Arrange the bread in the bottom of a bowl, pour the hot liquid on top, and serve immediately.

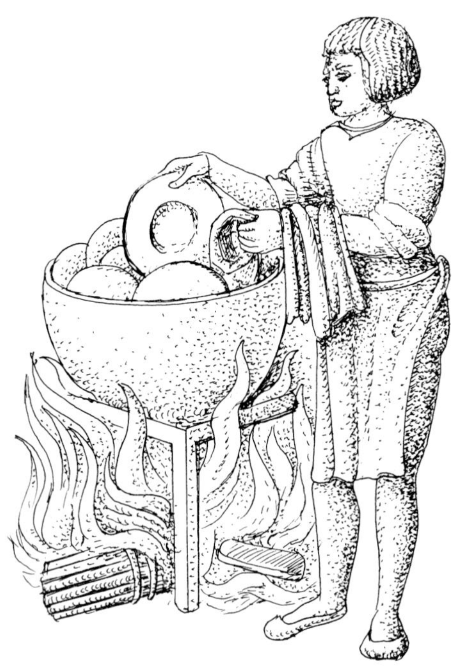

35. *Washing up* Washing up in a cauldron mounted on an iron trivet — based on a drawing by the antiquary Thomas Wright of 'one of the curious wooden sculptures in the church of Kirby Thorpe, in Yorkshire'.

For the cooks in all the royal kitchens, the serving of the meals by no means marked the end of their working day, for they had all their dirty pots, pans and spits to clean and scour ready for re-use. To start washing-up, some of the large kettles would have been filled with water and set over the fire to boil, hot water with either an alkaline lye made from wood ashes or, for more stubborn stains, the fine sand imported from Calais, being used with cloths to clean every utensil. As the fourteenth-century writer John Trevisa had observed, 'Brazen vessels by soon red and rusty, but they be oft scoured with sand, and have an evil savour and smell but they be tinned. Also brass, if it be without tin, burneth soon.[33] If the scullions cleaned too vigorously the tinning would be quickly removed and the working life of the pots would be considerably shortened:[34]

> No scouring for pride
> Spare kettle whole side
>
> Though scouring be needfull, yet scouring too much
> Is pride without profit, and robbeth thine hutch.
> Keep kettles from knocks, set tubs out of sun
> For mending is costly, and crackt is soon done.

9

Preparing for Dinner

Pantry and Cellars

When the cooks were busy in the kitchens, numerous other servants were fully occupied with their own preparations, largely in the rooms beneath and around the Great Hall.

In one small room beneath the screens passage (no. 56), cartloads of manchets and cheat loaves from the bread store in the bakehouse would be unloaded by the pages of the pantry.[1] The quality and quantity were then checked by the groom brever, who recorded their number by cutting notches on a split tally-stick, keeping one half for himself, and giving the other to the bakehouse staff. From here the bread was carried up to the pantry on the floor above, where the manchets would be stored in one set of bread bins, and after the pages had used their chipping knives to pare away the tough outer crusts, the cheat loaves into another.[2] One page for the King's mouth pared the cheat loaves from the privy bakehouse and took them with manchets up to the chambers, while the other pantry staff took the ordinary cheat bread into the Great Hall. In order to see that the bread weas efficiently and economically served, the yeomen brever and the pages took their meals in the pantry, and the grooms at the tables just inside the Hall. Next morning at eight the brever had to meet the clerk of the kitchens here, and present him with a precise account of how many loaves had been distributed the previous day.

The provision and serving of all the wines, ales and beers was the responsibility of William Abbott, sergeant of the cellar, constable of Cardigan Castle and keeper of the forest of Radnor.[3] To carry out his work he had

36. *The Great Cellar* Here, beneath the Great Watching Chamber, all the wine was kept for the household. A yeoman treyer would tap the casks when needed by boring a hole in the end with his auger and driving in the tap; he would use a gimlet to bore the hole in the top to receive the spile-pin.

three separate departments, the Cellar itself dealing with wine, the Buttery with ale and beer, and the Pitcher House with jugs, cups and serving. The barrels of wine purchased by the purveyors, or received as gifts, were stored either in the great wine cellar (no. 50), or, if for the King's use, in the adjacent privy cellar (no. 51), where they were checked and accounted for by the purveyors and set up on their stands, or 'stillages'.[4] Every day the groom grobber checked the barrels, and ensured that none were tapped by the yeoman treyer, unless a clerk comptroller was there to supervise the operation. Using a tarrier, or auger, a hole would be bored, pointing slightly upwards into the vertical end of the barrel, some four fingers' breadth up from the bottom of the rim, to receive a cannel, or tap. A gimlet was then used to pierce a smaller hole in the top of the barrel, into which a faucet or peg was driven.[5] This allowed air to enter as the wine was drawn off by the treyer, before he delivered it to the bar at the cellar door.[6]

The privy cellar was probably used for sweetening and spicing wine to make hippocras, the digestive taken by the King at the end of his meals. For small quantities, the spices were put into a conical filter-bag of felted woollen cloth – its shape supposedly resembled the sleeve of Hippocrates, the celebrated Greek physician. A pint (575ml) of wine was poured into the bag, followed by a pint of sweetened wine – then it was all poured back through the bag until it ran perfectly clear. For larger batches, beaten spices would be mixed in a gallon (4.5 litres) of wine in a pewter basin, and a sample run through the first two filter-bags in a row of six suspended from a bar; then the spicing of the main batch would be corrected as necessary and the whole batch passed through all six filters, after which it was poured into a vessel and sealed down until ready for use.[7]

HIPPOCRAS

1150ml (2pt) red or white wine
2.5ml ($\frac{1}{2}$ tsp) each of ground cloves, nutmeg and galingale
10ml (2 tsp) ground cinnamon
225g (8oz) sugar
1.5ml ($\frac{1}{4}$ tsp) ground ginger

1. *Mix the spices in the wine and leave overnight.*
2. *Filter the wine through a paper coffee-filter and run it through a second time if cloudy.*
3. *Dissolve the sugar in the filtered wine, ready for use.*

The malt liquors served at the palace included ale and beer: ale, the weaker brew, was probably still flavoured with herbs at this time. To ensure that the beer, the stronger, hopped drink, was well brewed, John Pope the King's beer brewer called upon continental expertise – he was allowed to retain twelve foreigners in his house 'meet for the said feat of beer brewing'.[8] The purveyors tasted the ales and beers at the brewhouse, and supervised the groom versours while they set the barrels on their stillages in the beer cellar (no. 53). From here the liquor was drawn into leather jugs that would then be passed out at the hatches of the privy buttery (no. 57) and the great buttery (no. 58), as called for.

The grooms of the pitcher house would carry the ale and beer from the butteries and the wines from the cellar bars upstairs, where they were served by yeomen of the pitcher house, using cups of the appropriate status issued to them by the sergeant of the cellar.[9] Since some of these would have been used to serve the bouche of court the previous evening, the pitcher house staff had to 'fetch them home' every morning, and carefully count them to check that none had gone missing and that there were enough for everyone at dinner. They were then washed ready for use, and dried with worn-out linen cloths supplied by the Ewery.

✿

The Ewery was the department that dealt with all the table linen and hand-washing equipment. It received its cloth by measure from the Counting House, and its silver or gilt basins and ewers, as well as napkins decorated with these precious metals, from either the Treasurer of the Household or the Jewel House, for use in the chambers and Hall.[10]

Just to the south of the Lord's-side kitchen and linked to it by a doorway lay the Scullery Yard (no. 37), the 'Little Court' used by the officers of the scullery. Except for the Henrician south wall it was all built by Cardinal Wolsey, probably soon after 1515. The Scullery was essentially the palace's hardware and tableware department. Its sergeant, clerk and twelve yeomen, grooms and 'children' were responsible for the purchase, safekeeping, maintenance and replacement of all the tubs, trays, baskets, flaskets, chests and standards used here, and the brass pots, pans, spits, oven-peels and so forth used by the kitchen staff, which cost an estimated £66 13s 4d each year.[11] They also bought in the 'herbs' used in the kitchen – this word then including vegetables of all kinds, rather than just the medicinal and flavouring plants we would now call herbs. These cost £40 a year.

Among his various duties, George Stonehouse, the clerk of the scullery at this time, had to record the supply of tableware used in the Hall and chambers.[12] Recasting and reworking the pewter vessels used in the Great Hall, incorporating the metal of those that had worn out or broken, reduced the cost of supplying the dishes by about half, but it still came to £40 a year. The pewter scullery (no. 36) was probably located on the west side of the Scullery Yard. From here timber-framed hatches were cut through Wolsey's brick walls into the hall-place dressers so that the dirty dishes returning from the Great Hall could be efficiently passed inside, all under the watchful eye of the clerks in the dresser office directly opposite.

The silver dishes issued from the Lord's-side dressers were supplied to the Scullery by the Jewel House. Having been used in the Council and Great Watching Chambers, they may have been returned through the same hatches as the pewter, but this seems unlikely because mixing up cheap pewter with expensive silver would make it very difficult to maintain its security and prevent it being damaged. However, the 1674 lodging survey describes the room at the south-west corner of the Great Space (no. 43) as the Lord Chamberlain's scullery. Its position in the Great Space, its large dresser hatch and its proximity to the Lord's-side kitchen dresser hatches

37. *The Scullery Yard* Built by Cardinal Wolsey shortly after 1515, this yard lies just to the south of the Lord's-side kitchen. The pewter scullery is in the building to the left, and the Lord's-side dresser office in the one to the right.

would certainly make it most suitable for issuing and receiving the silver dishes as they passed between the kitchens and the chambers.

The dishes would be washed and cleaned in the pewter and silver sculleries, the polishing material most probably being whiting, a soft ground and washed chalk, which was supplied in balls, the Althorpe accounts including payments for '12 balls of whiteing to scowre the plate'.[13] Made into a paste with a little water, and rubbed on with pieces of worn-out table-linen from the Ewery, it would polish with minimal scratching; the plate would then be rinsed and dried with clean cloths.[14]

10

Serving the King

A Royal Ceremony

By combining evidence from royal ordinances from Edward IV's to Edward VI's time, comparable household regulations and instruction manuals, it is possible to gain some idea of how the meals were served at the palace.

In a period when personal timekeeping devices were of the greatest rarity, and given that the faces of the astronomical clock in the central Gatehouse were not visible to all, it was essential to devise some foolproof method of informing everyone of mealtimes. For this reason the minstrels were instructed to go 'blowing and piping, to such offices as must be warned to prepare for the King and his household at metes and soupers, to be the more ready in all servyces, and all these sitting in the hall togedyr, wherof sume use trumpettes, sum shalmuse [shawms, instruments of the oboe class, with double reeds in a globular mouthpiece] and small pipes', and they were provided with 'a torch for wynter nyghts whyles they blowe to souper and other revelles'.[1] This tradition was continued by Elizabeth I – for whom twelve trumpeters and two kettle-drums made the Great Hall ring for a whole half-hour before the Yeomen of the Guard carried up her meals. Playing from the gallery over the screens entrance to the Great Hall, they could not fail to alert everyone in the neighbouring offices, while remaining well out of the way of bustling servants preparing the tables on the floor below.

Preparations for serving the King began with the sewer, the King's master cook and the doctor of physic together deciding his menu.[2] The surveyors of the dresser, Edward Weldon and Eustace Sulliard, then had to make sure that all the king's food was of the very best and that it was safely and cleanly handled from the time it was received from the larders by the master cook for the king's mouth through to its appearance at the dresser of the Privy Kitchen.[3]

In the 1540s Henry usually dined in private either in his Privy Chamber or in his secret lodgings – rooms for which neither the ordinances or any other source can provide any meaningful practical information. On some

38. *Serving the King* In this drawing, based on an original probably of the early seventeenth century, Henry VIII is being served by the staff of his Privy Chamber; the arrangement of the canopy of estate, the dais and the standing cupboard with its display of gold plate is clearly shown.

occasions, however, especially when he was entertaining ambassadors and other important guests, he used the Presence Chamber. Here his table would be set up, probably by the gentlemen ushers of the privy chamber clad in their livery coats, each of which took ten yards (9.1m) of crimson velvet.[4] George Villiers, sergeant of the ewery, or his yeoman ewerer for the King's mouth, would now lay a tablecloth of white linen worked in damask with flowers, knots, crowns or fleur-de-lis.[5] He also provided the damask linen towels and the magnificent ewers, lavers and basins used for hand-washing, all made of gold, gilt, glass or marble. One basin, for example, weighed a massive 332 ounces (9.4 kg) and incorporated a fountain in the form of three women who spouted water from their breasts.[6] In cold weather the groom for the King's mouth heated the water beforehand, in a chafing dish kept specially for this purpose.[7]

Now the sewer, Lord Thomas Grey, Sir Percival Hart or Sir Edward Warner, and the carver, Henry Howard, Earl of Surrey, Lord William Howard or Sir Francis Bryan, would be armed with linen towels, each measuring 9 feet 9 inches (nearly 3m) by four and a half inches (11cm) wide. The sewer would probably hang his around his neck like a stole, while the carver would place his over his left shoulder and knot it at his right hip before setting the salt, the trenchers, the gold-fringed napkin, the cutlery and the manchets from the pantry all in precise positions on the tablecloth.[8] All these utensils were of fabulous quality: the salts made of bejewelled and enamelled precious metals, or ivory, jasper, agate, beryl, chalcedony or rock crystal, and incorporated features such as clocks or fountains.[9] The trenchers were small silver, silver-gilt or marble plates, some with a recess for salt sunk into one corner.[10] Even the bread was wrapped in a 'cover-pain' of richly embroidered and gold-fringed linen, or brilliant orange and white silk fringed in white and gold.[11]

When the King informed the Chamber that he wished to dine, the sewer took the gentlemen ushers down to the privy kitchen dresser, returning with the first course in a procession which on days of estate was headed by a sergeant at arms, probably with his gilt mace, the Comptroller, the Treasurer, the Lord Great Master – all with their white sticks, the latter side by side with the Lord Chamberlain if he was present, then the sewer and the gentlemen ushers.[12] All the serving dishes were of massive silver gilt: chargers weighing around 80 ounces (2.3kg), platters in sets of twelve of around 35 to 50 ounces (990–1400g), and dishes, also in dozens, of around 25 to 30 oz (710–850g).[13] There were sets of twelve saucers, too – smaller, round vessels of about 8 to 12 ounces (225–350g), to hold mustard and similar sauces to accompany the main meats and fish. The first course would include pottages, brawn, stewed beef, mutton, pheasant, swan and capon, baked venison, blancmange, custard, jelly and fritters, for example, while the second comprised all manner of roast game, perch in jelly, doucets, leaches, cream of almonds and so on.[14] Having instructed the ushers where to place each of the dishes on the table, the sewer would go to the ewery table at one side of the Chamber and say to the ewerer, 'Give me a towel that the King shall wash with.' He would then lay the towel on his shoulder and go into the privy chamber, followed by an usher with a basin, then present the basin to the highest-ranking person present – an earl or baron on a day of estate – who then held it in front of the King as he washed.[15]

When the King had entered the Presence Chamber, attended by the Lord Chamberlain, and taken his seat at his table beneath the 'canopy of estate', everyone not directly involved in serving the meal, including the Lord Chamberlain, would leave the room.[16] Now the carver began his highly accomplished work. He had to know the particular way of carving each dish, how to cut it into pieces and place it on the King's trencher, and how to serve it with the appropriate sauces or other accompaniments. Using a carving set such as the 'case of lether with thre karvynge knives and a forke and viii meate knives thaftes [the hafts] white and grene garnished with metalle guilte' – one of thirty such sets owned by Henry VIII – the carver would take a knife, holding it between the thumb and first two fingers of his right hand. Then, being careful to use the correct terms and procedures when tackling each dish, he would carry out the specific operations, some of which are listed here:[17]

Meat	*Carving term*	*Action and sauce*
Brawn	leche	Slice, lay on a trencher, serve with mustard.
Venison	break	Slice, 12 cuts across with edge of knife, put in frumenty.
Pheasant	alay	Lift with left hand, remove wings, mince the meat into a syrup.
Goose	rear	Cut off legs, then wings, put legs at each side of separate platter, carve meat from the carcase, put it between legs and wings in the platter.
Hen	spoil	Cut off legs, then wings, mince wings, sprinkle with wine or ale 'for the sovereign'.
Hot pies		Remove lid.
Cold pies		Cut off crust from half-way up the sides.
Salmon	chyne	Slice into a dish, serve with mustard.
Haddock and cod	side	Cut down the back, remove bones, clean inside.
Baked herrings		Serve whole with salt and wine.
Salt fish		Remove bones and skin, serve with mustard.
Custard		Cut into 1 inch (2.5cm) squares.

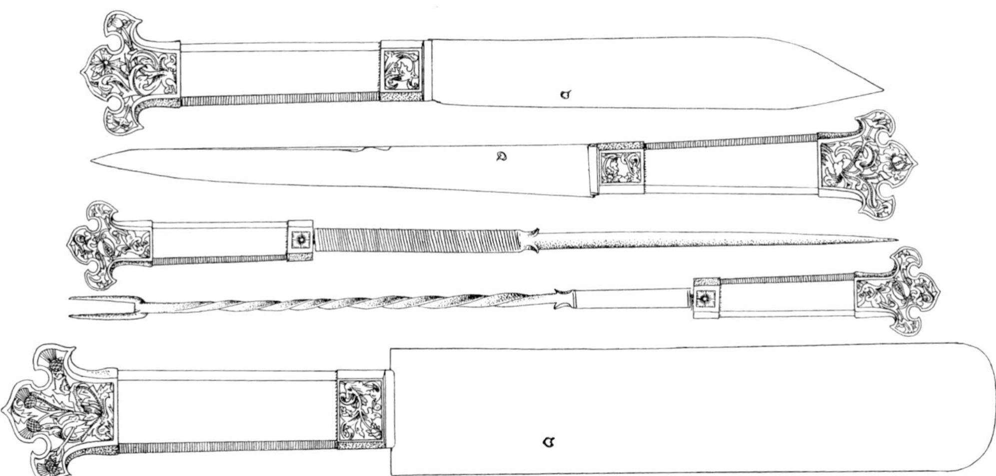

39. *A Carving Set* Henry VIII owned numerous carving sets, most of them housed in black leather cases. They may have resembled this German set of the late fifteenth century, which includes (top to bottom): a broad and a narrow carving knife, a sharpening steel, a serving fork, and a broad-bladed knife used either for serving or to scrape up crumbs from the tablecloth when 'voiding', or both.

The carver also undertook a little cooking at the table, using chafing dishes of silver gilt. Partridges, for example, had their legs and wings cut off and the flesh warmed with wine, ginger and salt in a dish set over glowing charcoal.[18] Other chafing dishes were 'gilt with hooles to roste Egges in, thandles and Feete of brasil, the chafingdishe foure squared having at everie corner a gilt pillor poiz [weighing] with the Brasil LXVII oz (1.9kg).[19] Served in this way, all the King's food appeared at his trencher ready for eating with the thumb and forefingers of his right hand, or, if soft or semi-liquid, his spoon. At his side he would find a manchet cut into fingers for eating with the other foods.

As for drink, the sergeant of the cellar, with his yeoman of the King's mouth, served wine and ale to the King's 'cupboard' after it had been brought up by the groom of the cellar to the King's mouth.[20] The cup-board – literally a 'cup-board' or table – looked very impressive with its display of vessels beautifully worked in gold, silver gilt and other precious materials. Wine would be placed here in matching pairs of flagons like those – 'well-chased, their bailes [handles] being Dolphyns fastened to the backes of a man and a woman, sitting upon the Baile a man holding in his hande a Cluster of grapes weying togethers DLXIIII oz [15 kg]'.[21] Here too were the cups made of gold, silver gilt, mother of pearl, ostrich eggs or porcelain; some were made for specific purposes, such as the gold malm-sey cups, the beer cups of alabaster, serpentine or silver and gilt, and the

assay cups used by the officers of the chamber to taste samples of water for washing or drink for the King's table before it was served by the cup-bearers.

Once the main courses had been served, any food or drink remaining on the table after the King had finished was 'saved and gathered by the officers of the almonry, and from day to day to be given to poore people at the utter court gate, by oversight of the under almoner, without diminishing, embesselling, or purloyning any part thereof, and neither in the chamber, nor other place where allowance of meate is had, the meate to be given away by anny sitting or wayting there'.[22] Tempting as they were, all these dishes from the King's table were to be given to the poor, the staff of the privy and presence chambers being provided with their own separate meals after the King had dined. One of the King's alms dishes, presumably for table service, was made of 314 ounces (8.9kg) of silver gilt, 'like a shippe, having two plain plates uppon the sides wherein the kinges armes is set'.[23] For state occasions it was borne by the Great Almoner, Dr Nicholas Heath, Bishop of Rochester, but at other times by John Batt, the under-almoner. Along with all the other food left over from the Council and Great Watching Chambers and the Great Hall, it would be carried down to the almonry (no. 55), close to the hall-place dresser, ready for distribution. Towards the end of the meal, probably after the second course, digestive dishes such as roast apples with caraway comfits, or cheese, were served, and then the remaining bread, napkins and tableware cleared away with due ceremonies. The carver next gathered together the crumbs and any scraps left on the cloth, using a broad-bladed 'voiding knife' and a shallow narrow-rimmed dish called a voider.[24]

Now the King would stand up, an usher kneeling before him to clean any crumbs form the skirts of his coat. It was at this point that the 'void' was served with the wafers brought here from the wafery, the hippocras prepared in the privy cellar, and all the spice dishes laden with comfits and dry and wet suckets prepared in the confectionary. It was for the latter that the King would use a fork, an implement used solely for eating ginger and similar preserves in syrup; it was not until the following century that the fork began to replace the fingers for eating meat and other foods. Henry VIII's inventory of 1547 lists both ginger forks and combined implements

40. *A Tudor napkin* The arms woven in the damask of this fine linen napkin are those used by both Henry VII and Henry VIII. The combined hunting- and food-based themes of the top panels, which show a huntsman blowing his horn, a hound and a deer, and a hunter with his spear approaching a boar, would certainly have appealed to Henry VIII.

with 'one spone with suckett forke at thende of silver and gilt poiz one oz iii quarters [45g]'.[25]

A sewer and a gentleman usher now brought a linen surnap and a towel from the ewery table, these having been carefully folded together in the form of a rectangular concertina. The surnap, as the name suggests, was designed to cover the napery, and was simply a long white linen cloth; the towel was another long piece of linen damask, worked with lovers' knots or fleur-de-lis and measuring some twenty-seven inches (68.5cm) wide.[26] Placing these on the table end to the King's right, the usher would put his rod inside the surnap and towel and walk down the front of the table, drawing them out across the tablecloth and reverencing the King when he was directly before him; then he would proceed a few feet beyond the far end of the table and kneel there, while supporting his end of the surnap and towel. Back at his end of the table, the sewer now knelt and firmly gripped his end of the surnap and towel, so that the usher could stretch them taut and fold the overhanging end up on to the table. Then he would rise, walk before the King to his right side, and slip his rod beneath the surnap and towel to form a single loose pleat called an estate. Passing before the King with a further reverence, he made a similar estate to the King's left before returning to his end of the table, kneeling and straightening the towel once more. Having completed these duties, he again carried his rod before the King, reverenced him, and returned to his place. Now the nobles bearing the ewer and basin approached, so that the King could wash his hands and dry them on the towel. To complete this whole ceremony, the usher slipped his rod into the folded towel and surnap at his end and pulled them along towards the King, while the sewer brought up his end at the same time so that towel and surnap were gathered together for the sewer to take back to the ewery table.[27] Finally, the dining table itself was dismantled and taken away, leaving the King standing beneath his canopy of estate ready to resume his activities.

This sketch of Henry VIII at table – which would apply to the Queen too – lacks many details, especially when compared with late fifteenth and early sixteenth century descriptions of noble and archbishoply dining ceremonies that set out every movement of the servants and tableware, but it does give some impression of the formality and magnificence of Tudor royal dining habits.

Even when the King dined away from the Presence Chamber his table there was still served with the King's service, but it was now the Lord Chamberlain who ate there, with lords spiritual and temporal above the level of baron – barons were admitted only if insufficient numbers of higher nobility were present at court.[28]

11

Dining in Chamber and Hall

Etiquette and Ritual

The Lord Great Master, with a number of other lords, dined in the King's Council Chamber, where they were attended by two of his gentlemen, a gentleman usher, a sewer, the hamperman, and grooms and pages of the chamber, with one yeoman usher to guard his door and another to bring up the food from the Lord's-side dressers. All these servants ate the food left after the nobles had dined at 10 a.m. and taken their supper four hours later.[1]

The Lord Chamberlain, meanwhile – unless dining in the Presence Chamber – took his meals in the Great Watching Chamber with other lords and ladies, the Vice-Chamberlain and the Captain of the Guard, as well as the King's cupbearers, carvers and sewers, esquires for the body, gentleman ushers and sewers of the chamber who were not on duty that day. Here they were served by a gentleman usher, a sewer, a groom and pages of the chamber, a yeoman of the chamber to bring up the food from the Lord's-side dresser, and an usher to guard the door. All of these later dined on the food left after the senior officers had departed.[2]

In the Great Watching Chamber and the other, smaller, chambers where specified officers such as the Master of the Horse, the Captain of the Gentlemen Pensioners, the Secretaries and the servants of the King's and Queen's Privy Chambers took their meals, there would be far less ceremony. Serving and eating habits here were probably just like those to be found every day in any noble dining chamber. Good table manners would be *de rigueur*, especially since everyone dining here would have been sent away from home when quite young to be a servant in a household of equal or superior status to his own, in order to gain those polite accomplishments which would elevate him from the lower orders for the rest of his days.

41. *Dining in Chamber* There are no contemporary illustrations of the nobles dining in the Council and Great Watching Chambers, but this detail shows them being served in a tent at 'The Field of the Cloth of Gold'. It is interesting to speculate whether the figure at the end of the table is Charles Brandon, Duke of Suffolk and Lord Great Master. It bears a certain resemblance to him, and his appearance here, close to the unique representations of the Kitchen, Boiling House, Bakehouse and Buttery which he controlled, would be most appropriate.

When meals were to be served in the Great Watching Chamber, the tables would be set up by the pages, who may have stored them in their adjacent pages' chamber when not in use. Since the tables were only set up at mealtimes, they lacked the thick tops and solid frames of later periods, but instead would have relatively light planked tops, supported at intervals on trestles. Each trestle had one horizontal bar into which three mortices were cut, one at one end and two at the other, at slightly outward-splaying angles. Once the tenoned ends of the three legs had been inserted in the mortices, each trestle stood really firm on the floor, but once the weight of the table-top had been removed the legs could be easily pulled out, reducing the trestle to four short, interchangeable bars ideal for stacking in any convenient place[3]

The yeoman and groom ewerers for the King's mouth then laid the cloth and prepared the ewery board for hand-washing, leaving the gentleman usher to supervise the setting of the table with silverware, rather than the gold used by the King, brought up from the scullery.[4] Manchet and cheat loaves now arrived from the pantry, wine, beer and ale from the butteries, and the food from the Lord's-side dresser. Contemporary books of manners suggest that on taking their places, the Lord Chamberlain and his companions would have found everything they needed set out before them.[5] The silver trenchers – or shallow plates – probably had smaller flat, round wooden trenchers placed inside them to provide a good cutting service and also to protect the polished silver from serious damage. One contemporary set ordered for Sir Thomas Brudenell was described as having 'round trenchers of silver . . . of 6 ounces [175g] the piece . . . to lay a wooden trencher in the midst, as ye know the manner is, and about the edge would be some pretty print or work'.[6] To the right of the trencher would lie a silver spoon, and perhaps a narrow, sharp-pointed eating knife – although it was customary for everyone to carry his own in a sheath hung from his belt – and above it, a drinking cup of silver or perhaps fine Venetian glass. To the left lay a manchet loaf and a fine linen damask napkin measuring some 45 by 27 inches (114 by 68.5cm), folded two or three times along its length and then probably crosswise to form a neat rectangle.[7]

After grace, each diner opened his napkin into a long strip and placed it either over his left shoulder or across his left forearm, for its purpose was simply to dry the lips before and after drinking rather than as a protective overall for messy eaters. He would then pick up his manchet or cheat loaf in his left hand, place it on his trencher, slice it horizontally through the middle, cut the top into four strips and reassemble it back in its place as if was whole, and then cut the bottom into three strips and similarly reassemble it crust uppermost alongside.[8] When the pottage arrived, he spooned it up from the communal dish served to each mess. He might break off a piece of bread and dip it into the dish to absorb the liquid, then eat it with the spoon, but bread could not be crumbled into the dish because this would spoil it for others.[9] Once each diner had taken his share of the pottage he would clean his spoon with a piece of bread, which he would then eat, leaving the spoon clean for eating other dishes.

When the main course arrived, he used the same method for eating the semi-liquid dishes, for the rich gravy accompanying roasts and for the succulent juice-soaked 'sops', or bread cubes, on which many meats and fish were presented. For vegetables and cereals such as frumenty or rice, he could spoon a quantity on to his trencher, to accompany the meats, always being careful to wipe the spoon clean on a piece of bread before moving on from one dish to another. Solid dishes of meat and fish, which came to the table in mess-sized joints, required a different approach – identical to that used by the carver at ceremonial meals.[10]

The matter of greatest importance was the use of the right and left hands. In essence, only the left hand could touch the communal dishes, leaving the right solely for gripping the personal knife or spoon or for lifting food to the lips with the fingers.[11] In this way there could be no risk of any dish being contaminated by anyone's saliva. When a joint was served to a mess, the diners, probably giving precedence to the senior amongst them, took hold of the piece they wanted with the thumb and first two fingers of the left hand, cut it from the joint using their knife similarly held with the thumb and first two fingers of the right hand, the butt inside the palm. Still gripping it with the left hand, they would place the piece of meat on their trencher, holding it there until they had cut it up into small mouthfuls. If salt was required, it was lifted from the salt-cellar on the point of the knife and laid in a small heap on the trencher.[12] Prepared sauces such as mustard, served in open saucers, may have been taken in a similar way. Now the knife was cleaned with a piece of bread, as usual, and set down at the trencher, leaving the thumb and first two fingers of the right hand free to pick up each piece of meat in turn, dip it in the salt or sauce on the trencher, and lift it to the lips.

Pies would be eaten in a similar manner. Holding the edge of the crust with the thumb and first two fingers of the left hand, the diner would make one cut from the centre of the pie to the left of his fingers and a second from half an inch (1.3cm) short of the centre to the right of his fingers, then lift the slice on to his trencher. The next diner followed suit, proceeding anticlockwise around the pie, so that no one handled anyone else's piece and everyone took the same proportion of crust to filling. This precise information does not come from any Tudor source, however, but from descriptions of late nineteenth and early twentieth century practice in East Yorkshire farmhouses, where good medieval table manners survived intact for centuries. Pennine weavers were spooning up their pottage from communal bowls certainly up to the 1880s, and even within the last few years one could be set at table in some North Yorkshire farms without any cutlery at the place-setting because the personal clasp-knife was still used for eating such items as meat and cheese.[13] Any bones or other debris accumulating on the trencher were deposited in a dish called a voider placed on the table for this purpose. Thus, by constantly cleaning the knife, spoon and trencher with pieces of bread it was possible to eat elegantly, conve-

42. *Place-settings* The upper table is set with silver for a noble dining in the Chamber: a wooden trencher is set in his plate, his napkin and a manchet, cut in pieces, are to the left, his cup and wine flagon to the right, and a dish of food and a saucer of sauce before him. In contrast, the servant dining in the Great Hall (below) has a simple ash trencher, a pared cheat loaf and napkin to his left, his wooden drinking bowl and a leather jug of ale to his right, and a mess of pottage and a saucer of mustard ready to be shared with the other three who comprised his mess.

niently and cleanly. To those who have demonstrated it over the past decade, it is easy to understand why it remained popular for centuries and why that Italian affectation, the fork, took so long to be accepted by the general body of English society.

Having moved on to the fruit, the Lord Chamberlain and his companions would finally have washed their hands and left the table. Their servants now took their places, and there would be very little left-over food for the almoner to remove from the Great Watching Chamber after they had finished eating.

43. *The Great Hall* Bare of tapestries, heated by its central fireplace and buzzing with hundreds of lower courtiers and household servants, this is how the Great Hall appeared at dinner and supper every day, unless it was required for some rare royal entertainment.

❂

Down in the body of the Great Hall (no. 40), it is probable that the tables remained standing throughout the court's stay at the palace, to be dismantled only if this space was required for a great ceremony or entertainment. This may account for the fact that the household regulations state that they were to be brushed clean by two groom ewerers before they laid their cloths. Tables for hall use could be sixteen feet (4.8m) or more in length but only two feet (60cm) broad, since wider tables would not only occupy more space but would also prevent the diners who sat along each side from conveniently eating from communal dishes such as pottage.[14] With fourteen tables of this type, each holding, say, twenty-four people as six messes, the Great Hall could readily seat 336 people in 84 messes, while still leaving room for the waiters and others and for the large central fireplace, its sole method of heating.

Each tablecloth would overhang the edges of the table by some seven to twelve inches (17.5–30cm), and would be changed at least twice a week – more often if soiled.[15] As well as laying the cloths, the two yeomen and two groom ewerers for the hall, assisted by their page, set out the ewers and basins, probably of pewter, and also the linen towels, on a ewery table in an area called 'the Towel' close to the entrance screen. Here, while everyone in the Hall was eating too, the groom ewerers for the hall took their meals, along with the other servants who served there, so that they could quickly supply any needs as they occurred. All this was supervised by the marshal of the hall, or one of his ushers, the officers responsible for maintaining good order here.

At each place in the Great Hall a napkin would be provided by the Ewery, along with a cheat loaf set out by the groom or yeoman of the pantry, a trencher in the form of a disc of ash-wood some seven inches (17.5cm) in diameter, with a convex bead turned around its edge, a pewter spoon, and a wooden drinking cup set out by the yeoman of the pitcher house. In addition, the pantry staff would set out a pewter salt cellar to each mess.[16] In theory, the manners and service here, if not the quality and range of the food and drink, should have been as good as those in the Great Watching Chamber. In practice, however, it was much more boisterous, the servants dining here lacking the polish of their superiors. Contemporary descriptions of dining in the Hall, although obviously satirical, provide colourful evidence of the behaviour encountered there.

The tables were so crowded that the servants frequently spilled broth, liquor or fat over the diner's clothes and hats, as they reached over them to put dishes on the table. Then, instead of observing gentlemanly reserve, everyone would dig in:[17]

If the dish is pleasant, either flesh or fish,
Ten hands at once swarm in the dish.
And if it be flesh, ten knives shalt thou see
Mangling the flesh and in the platter flee:
To put there thy hands is peril without fail,
Without a gauntlet or else a glove of mail.
Amongst all these knives thou one of both must have,
Or else it is hard thy fingers whole to save:
Oft in such dishes in court is seen,
Some leave their fingers, each knife is so keen.
On finger gnaweth some hasty glutton,
Supposing it is a piece of beef or mutton . . .

There was good reason for this haste, for although,[18]

Slowe be the servers in serving in alway,
But swift be they after taking meat away.
A special custom is used them among,
No good dish to suffer on board to be long.
The hungry servers which at the table stand
At every morsel hath eye unto thy hand . . .
Because that thy leavings is only their part,
If thou feed thee well, sore grieved is their heart;
Namely of a dish costly and daintious,
Each piece that thou cuttest to them is tedious.
Then at the cupboard one doth another tell
'See how he feedeth, like a devil of Hell,
Our part he eateth, nought good shall we taste',
Then pray to god it will be thy last.

The serving of ale caused similar problems. It was brought up from the great buttery by the yeomen of the pitcher house in leather jugs, which cost £5 a year in replacements.[18] Each mess received twelve pints per meal each meat day (six pints per man per day), and eight pints per meal on fish days (or four pints per man per day). It was poured out into wooden cups, these being shaped like open bowls rather than as modern cups. Turned from tough ash, they cost £20 a year in replacements. Each morning the yeomen and page of the pitcher house had to retrieve all those that had been used to serve liveries to bedchambers the previous night, carefully counting them to ensure that there were sufficient to serve the Hall.[19] Some smaller cups, perhaps holding about a pint, were used individually, but most people appear to have shared a common drinking bowl to each

44. *The Buttery bar* With typical attention to good housekeeping, the cellar staff within the buttery were kept separate from the pitcher house staff who carried up the ale and wine and served it, thus ensuring that there was little opportunity for unauthorised consumption.

mess, which even then was considered unsavoury as well as unfair – anyone calling for more ale if their bowl had been drained by others was called 'malapart or dronke, or an abbey lowne [worthless, idle monk], or limnier [manuscript illuminator] of a monke'. By repute, the cups were scoured only once a year, being merely swilled at other times. Not surprising, then, that they appeared:[20]

> Old, black and rusty, lately taken from some sink:
> And in such vessel drink thou often time,
> Which in the bottom is full of filth and slime,
> And in that vessel thou drinkest oft I wis,
> In which some states [important men] or dames late did piss.

But for those who dined here every day such matters would have been of little concern, for theirs was a canteen culture of the most robust kind. Once they had finished, got up, washed and returned to their duties, the

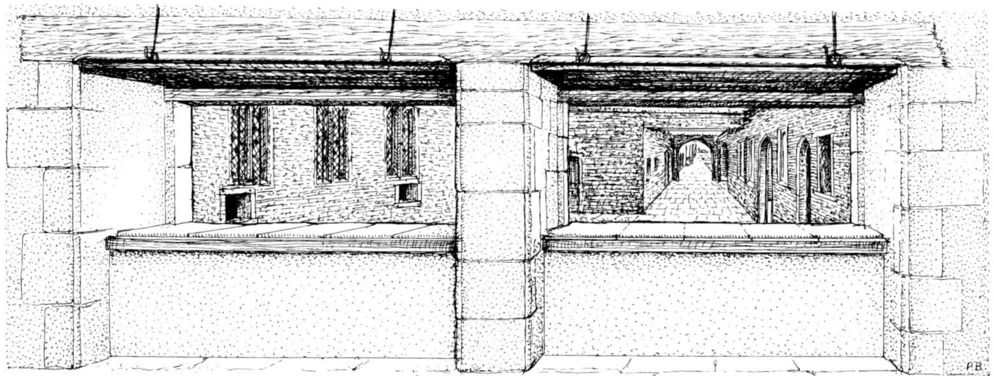

45. *The Hall-place dresser* When dinner was served, every dish would be taken from these hatches, carried to the dresser-office hatch to the immediate right, and then up into the Great Hall. On return, the waste food was deposited in the Almonry directly ahead, and the dishes and so forth passed into the pewter scullery through the square hatches on the left, all under the watchful eyes of the clerks in the dresser office.

servers would dine on the left-overs and whatever they had managed to put to one side, then carry all the dishes and tableware down to the hatches in the pewter scullery wall, by the hall-place dresser office (no. 34). Any remaining food would go into the almonry here (no. 55), and then be taken to the poor waiting at the gate of the Outer Court, where it had arrived fresh and raw perhaps a day, or even a matter of hours, before.

Although noteworthy textual research was undertaken by a number of mid-Victorian scholars, it is only in recent years that historic kitchens and domestic management have begun to be studied in any detail, and only now that the sophistication of their design and administration is being slowly revealed. In the Tudor kitchens at Hampton Court we find a domestic organisation that is both conceptually and physically second to none. Not only are they the finest kitchens of their period, but they are the largest, most intact and best documented of all Britain's early industrial buildings – a virtually faultless management scheme realised in brick, stone and timber. If the opportunity arises, go and see them for yourself, following the public route through to the Back Gate, and on towards the dressers, observing how each building, door, window and fireplace has been arranged for maximum efficiency. Then move on to the Great Hall and the Great Watching Chamber, and see where the dinners and suppers were served in interiors of the greatest magnificence. It is a truly incomparable experience.

BIBLIOGRAPHY

A.W. *The Booke of Cookry Very Necessary for all Such as Delight Therein* (1584), 1591

Adams, J. *The History of the Worshipful Company of Blacksmiths*

Adams, S. *Household Accounts and Disbursement Books of Robert Dudley, Earl of Leicester, 1558–1561, 1584–1586*, Camden 5th series (Cambridge, 1995).

Aitken, L. *Memoirs of the Court of Queen Elizabeth (1819)*

Aitken, M., Carter, A. and Evans, D.H. 'Excavations in Norwich 1971–78 Part II', *East Anglian Archaeology, xxvi*

Alan, P.S. *Selections from Erasmus* (1918)

Anon. *A Closet for Ladies & Gentlewomen* (1608), 1611

The Boke of Cokery (c.1500)

The boke of kervynge (1508)

The Good Hous-wives Treasurie (1588)

Antiquarian Repertory (1775)

Ashmole, E. *The Institution, Laws & Ceremonies of the most Noble Order of the Garter* (1672)

Austin, T. *Two Fifteenth Century Cookery Books*, Early English Text Society, OS xci (1899)

Barkeley, A. *A Ship of Fooles* (1509) (ed.) T.H. Jameson (1874), ii, 90–4

'The Cytezen and Uplondyshman' (c. 1524), ed. F.W. Fairholt, *Percy Society*, xxxi (1848)

Boorde, A. *A Dyetary of Helth* (1542) ed. F.J. Furnivall, Early English Text Society, extra series x (1870)

Brand, J. *The Everyday Book* (1827)

Brears, P. *Traditional Food in Yorkshire* (Edinburgh, 1987)

Northcountry Folk Art (Edinburgh, 1989)

'Rare Conceits & Strange Delights' in C.A. Wilson, *Banquetting Stuffe* (Edinburgh, 1991), 66–114

'Wassail! Celebrations in Hot Ale' in C.A. Wilson, *Liquid Nourishment* (Edinburgh, 1993), 106–41

'Transparent Pleasures', *Petit Propos Culinaires*, liii (1996), 8–19

Ryedale Recipes (Hutton le Hole and Beverley, 1998)

A Taste of Leeds (Derby, 1998)

Browne, Sir T. *Norfolk Birds* (1682) in *Works* (1835), iv

Buttes, H. *Dyets Dry Dinner* (1599)

Carew, R. *Survey of Cornwall* (1602)

Cavendish, G. *The Life of Cardinal Wolsey* (1893), 1962

Cogan, T. *The haven of Health* (1584), 1636

Colman, L. (ed.) *Alexandre Dumas' Dictionary of Cuisine* (1959)

Dawson, T. *The Good huswifes Jewell* (1587), 1597

Digby, Sir K. *The Closet of Sir Kenelm Digby Knight Opened* (1669), reprinted 1910 with introduction by A. Macdonall

Dugdale, Sir W. *Originales Judiciales* (1671)

Earle, J. *Microcosmographie* (1628)

Elyot, Sir T. *The Castel of Helth* (1541

Emmison, F.G. *Tudor Food and Pastimes* (1964)

Fairholt, F.W. 'On an Inventory of Sir Thomas Ramsey', *Archaeologia*, xl (1846), 332

Frere, C.F. (ed.) *A Proper Newe Booke of Cokerye* (Cambridge, 1913)

Furnivall, F.J. *Early English Meals & Manners* (1868)

Gage, H. *The History of Antiquities of Hengrave in Suffolk* (1822)

Giustianino, S. *Four Years at the Court of Henry VIII* (1854)

Groos, D. *The Diary of Baron Waldstein* (1981)

Harrison, W. *Elizabethan England*, ed. F.J. Furnivall and L. Washington (1902)

Hieatt, C.B. and Butler, S. *Curye on Inglysch*, Early English Text Society (1985)

Hodgett, G.A.J. (ed.) *Stere Htt Well* (Adelaide, n.d.)

Hollingshead, R. *Holinshed's Chronicles of England, Scotland and Ireland* (1808)

Jaine, T. *Building a Wood-fired Oven* (Totnes, 1996)

Johnson, B. *The Fountaine of Self-love or Cynthias Revels* (1600)

Knell, D. 'Tudor Furniture from the *Mary Rose*', *Regional Furniture*, ix (1997), 74

Law, E. *The History of Hampton Court Palace in Tudor Times* (1885)

Loades, D. *The Tudor Court* (1992)

Lorwin, M. *Dining with William Shakespeare* (New York, 1976)

Markham, G. *The English Hus-wife* (1615)

May, R. *The Accomplish't Cook* (1600), 1685 edn.

McNeil, F.M. *The Scots Kitchen* (1963)

Murrell, J. *A Delightful Daily Exercise for ladies & Gentlewomen* (1621)

Murrell's Two Books of Cookrie (1638)

Nicholas, N.H. *The Privy Purse Expenses of King Henry the Eighth* (1827)

Nott, J. *The Cook's Dictionary* (1726)

Owen, G. *The Description of Pembrokeshire* (1693), 1891

Partridge, J. *The Treasurie of Commodious Conceits and Hidden Secrets* (1573)

The Widowes Treasure (1585)

Plat, Sir H. *Delightes for Ladies* (1602) reprinted 1948 with introduction by G.E. and K.R. Fussell

Ruscelli, G. *The Secretes of the Reverend Maister Alexis of Piedmont* (1562)
Rye, W.B. *England as seen by Foreigners* (1865)
Scappi, B. *Opera di Bartolommeo Scappi cuoce secreto di Papa Pio V* (Rome, 1570)
Seager, H.W. *Natural History in Shakespeare's Time* (Chicheley, 1972)
Simon, A. *Birds and their Eggs* (1994)
A Concise Encyclopaedia of Gastronomy: VII, Meat (1945)
The Star Chamber Dinner Accounts (1959)
Simpkinson, J.N. *The Washingtons, a tale of a country parish in the 17th century, based on authentic documents* (App. 1593–1645) (1860)
Sneyd, C.A. *A Relation . . . of the Island of England*, Camden Society, xxxvi (1847)
Spry, C. and Hume, R. *The Constance Spry Recipe Book* (1969)
Spurling, H. (ed.) *Elinor Fettiplace's Receipt Book* (1986)
Strutt, T. *Manners, Customs . . . of the Inhabitants of England* (1774)
Thurley, S. The Sixteenth-century Kitchens at Hampton Court' *Journal of the British Archaeological Association*, cxliii (1990)
Royal Palaces of Tudor England (Yale, 1993)
Trevisa, J. *Bartholomeus de Proprietatibus Rerum* (1535)
Tusser, T. *Five Hundred Points of Good Husbandry* (1557), 1812 ed.
Venner, T. *Via Recta ad Vitam Longam* (1620)
W.M. *A Queen's Delight*, 1671 edn
Walcot, M.E.C. 'Inventories & Valuations of religious Houses . . .' *Archaeologia*, xlii, 2nd series (1871)
Watkin, D. *The Royal Interiors of Regency England* (1984)
Wilson, C.A. *Food and Drink in Britain* (London, 1976)
Winchester, B. *Tudor Family Portrait* (1995)
Wriothesley, C. *A Chronicle of England 1485–1599*, Camden Society NS xx (1877)
Young, J. *Sixteenth Century England*, Penguin History of Britain (1984)

NOTES

Abbreviations

BM	British Museum
C SP Span	*Calendar of Letters, Documents and State Papers relating to Negotiations between England and Spain* . . . ed. G.A. Bergenroth, P. D. Goyanyos, G. Mattingley and R. Tyler (1862–1965)
C SP Ven	*Calendar of State Papers and Manuscripts Relating to English Affairs Existing in the Archives and Collections of Venice* . . . ed. R.L. Brown, C. Cavendish-Bentinck, H.F. Brown and A.B. Hinds (1864–1940)
DNB	*Dictionary of National Biography*
HO	*A Collection of Ordinances and Regulations for the Government of the Royal Household*, Society of Antiquaries (1790)
IKH	*Inventory of King Henry VIII: the Transcript*, ed. D. Starkey (1988)
L & P	*Letters & Papers Foreign & Domestic, of the Reign of Henry VIII*, ed. S.J. Brewer, 2nd edn (1861–3)
OED	*Oxford English Dictionary*
PRO	Public Record Office

For other references, see the Bibliography.

Introduction

1. Delia Smith in Hodgett, introduction.
2. *CSP Ven*, 7/7/1517.

Chapter 1 The Counting House

1. *HO* 17–18.
2. *HO* 63.
3. PRO E36/241, f. 360.
4. *HO* 56.
5. *HO* 58.
6. *HO* 228.
7. *HO* 213, 211.
8. *HO* 162.
9. *HO* 69.
10. *HO* 175, 191.
11. *HO* 193–4, 197.
12. *HO* 230–1.
13. *HO* 211.
14. *HO* 231.
15. *HO* 224, 226.
16. *HO* 62.
17. Barkeley (1874), II, 90–4.
18. *HO* 228.
19. *HO* 231.
20. PRO LC6/202, ff. 148–50, 157, transcribed in Thurley (1990), 26–5.
21. *HO* 229, 236.
22. *HO* 238.
23. *HO* 62.
24. *HO* 62, 236.
25. *HO* 237.
26. *HO* 237.
27. *HO* 230.
28. *HO* 67–8.

Chapter 2 Serving the Court

1. *HO* 174, 191.
2. *HO* 185–90.
3. Wriothesley.
4. *HO* 191.
5. See *DNB*, Barkeley; Barkeley (1848), xl–xlii.
6. *HO* 191.
7. *HO* 171.
8. *HO* 177–90.
9. *HO* 174–5.
10. *C SP Span*, XIII, 31.

Chapter 3 The Outer Court

1. Thurley (1990), 22.
2. *HO* 220–1.
3. Sneyd, 10.
4. Simon (1944), 68–9.
5. Elyot, 31.
6. Venner, iii, 64.
7. Browne, 319.
8. Venner, 62.
9. Simon (1944), 54; *OED*, Puffin.
10. Carew, 35b.
11. Simon (1959), 13.
12. Simon (1944), 8.
13. Buttes, 137–8.
14. Shakespeare, W., *Henry the Eighth*, Act 3 Scene 2 lines 279–82.
15. Elyot, 21.
16. Brears (1989), 109.
17. Boorde, 270; Buttes, 137–8.
18. Buttes, 137.
19. Wilson, 118.
20. *HO* 220.
21. *HO* 223.
22. *HO* 237, 231.
23. Spry and Hume, 632.
24. *HO* 68–70, 140, 232.
25. *HO* 237, 231; *L&P 1545*, I, 856; *1544*, I, 1023.
26. *HO* 282, 209.
27. *L&P 1546*, I, 774.
28. *HO* 69.
29. Markham, 126.
30. *HO* 195.
31. Markham, 126; *HO* 69.
32. Jaine, 69–94; Seager, 304.
33. *HO* 195.
34. Boorde, 261.
35. *HO* 69, 194.
36. *HO* 238, 213, 196, 35.

37. *L&P 1541*, p. 766; *1543*, I, 623/20; *1545*, I, 612, 259, 846 (1).
38. *HO* 196.
39. *HO* Act 43, Eliz I, cap. 14.
40. *HO* 162.
41. *HO* Thurley (1993), 230.
42. Allan, 126.
43. *C SP Ven*, II, 219.
44. Anon. (1775), II, 190; Rye, 101–13; Jonson, ii, 5.
45. Brears (1989), 179–89.
46. Nicholas, 12/12/1529.
47. *HO* 63, 175, 121.

Chapter 4 The Greencloth Yard

1. *L&P 1544*, I, 275, 1023; *HO* 239.
2. *HO* 65.
3. *HO* 42.
4. Nicholas, 11–13/5/1530; Cavendish (1893), 183.
5. *HO* 196.
6. *HO* 227.
7. *HO* 144.
8. Thurley (1990), 18.
9. Groos, 152.
10. *HO* 234–5.
11. Boorde, 80–9.
12. *L&P 1540*, 220 (36); *1544*, I, 1035 (116); *HO* 285.
13. Fairholt, 332.
14. *HO* 82.
15. *HO* 15.
16. *HO* 195.
17. *HO* 162.
18. *IKH* 6000–1.
19. Nicholas, 18/3/1531.
20. Anon. (1775), II, 190.
21. e.g. 'cotton wick for candles 18d' recorded in 1560; Emmison, 64.
22. *HO* 82.
23. *HO* 114.
24. *IKH* 1184.
25. *L&P 1545*, I, 465 (10); *HO* 75.
26. Boorde, 271.
27. Tusser, 49.
28. Brears (Derby 1998), 15.
29. Brears (Hutton 1998), 19.
30. Thurley (1990), 32.
31. *L&P 1544*, I, 275, 1023; *HO* 239.

Chapter 5 The Pastry Yard

1. PRO E36/241, ff. 581–2.
2. Tusser, 190.
3. *HO* 225.
4. *HO* 289.
5. *HO* 196.
6. *HO* 175.
7. Owen, 42.
8. Hieatt and Butler, 75; Austin, 99.
9. May, 331; Nott, 'Calver Salmon'.
10. Boorde, 142.
11. *HO* 196, 76.
12. Seager, 213.
13. Buttes, 211.
14. Anon. (1508).
15. Austin, 110.
16. Austin, 109.
17. Austin, 109; Hieatt and Butler, 213.
18. Young, 144.
19. Giustianino, June 1518, 193.
20. *HO* 81.
21. Nicholas.
22. *HO* 81.
23. *IKH* 1118.
24. Anon. (1508); Hieatt and Butler, 151; *HO* 81.
25. Plat, 42.
26. Hieatt and Butler, 152.
27. Partridge (1573).
28. Dawson, II, 37.
29. Boorde, 286.
30. Partridge (1585).
31. Adams, S., 145.
32. Plat, 31; Brears (1991), 109.
33. Dawson, II, 76.
34. Partridge (1585).
35. Brand, II, 497.
36. Dugdale, 132.
37. Anon. (1775), III, 244–6.
38. Ashmole, 603.
39. *HO* 450.
40. Cavendish (1962), 103; Lorwin, 388.
41. Cavendish (1962), 102–3.
42. Plat, 38.
43. Hieatt and Butler, 152.
44. Dawson (1597), 39.
45. Hieatt and Butler, 153; Murrell (1621); Spurling, 107–9.
46. Hieatt and Butler, 153.
47. Partridge (1585).
48. Plat, 27.
49. Murrell (1621).
50. Plat, 13.
51. Anon. (1611), 26.
52. Anon. (1611), 33; W.M. (1671), 69.
53. Ruscelli; Dawson, II, 39.
54. A.W., 32.
55. Plat, 29.
56. *L&P 1540/41*, 124; *1542*, 66; *1543*, II, 530; *1544*, I, 1023.
57. Nicholas, 14/8/1530, 14/6/1531.
58. Simon (1959), 79.
59. Partridge (1585).
60. Frere, 19.
61. Partridge (1585); Markham, 68.
62. A.W., 24.
63. Frere, 29.
64. Nicholas, 21/3/1530; Partridge, (1585).
65. Frere, 37.
66. Frere, 37.
67. A.W., 28.
68. Frere, 39.
69. Frere, 41.
70. Dawson, 17.
71. PRO E36/237, f. 442.

Chapter 6 The Paved Passage

1. *HO* 297.
2. Plat, 79.
3. L&P 1543, II, 530.
4. *L&P 1541*, 947 (26); *1544*, ii, 960 (27); *1543*, ii, 530.
5. *HO* 62.
6. *HO* 288, 296. These details of the Larder fees include the feet and belly-pieces of each ox, even though HO 297 states that they had already been taken by the Acatery. Presumably the

officers concerned understood the workings of the apparent anomaly.
7. *HO* 279.
8. *HO* 226–7.
9. *HO* 224.
10. *HO* 296.
11. *HO* 237.
12. Walcot, 222, 224.
13. Thurley (1990), 16.
14. *HO* 288.
15. *HO* 296.
16. Boorde, 262.
17. Markham, 47.
18. Hodgett, 29.

Chapter 7 The Hall-place and Lord's-side Kitchens

1. Earle.
2. *L&P 1541*, 878 (58), 141, 1226 (24).
3. *HO* 148.
4. *L&P 1541*, 140.
5. *L&P 1540*, 123b, 163b.
6. *HO* 69.
7. *HO* 174–92.
8. Aitken.
9. Hieatt and Butler.
10. May, Introduction.
11. Watkin, 17.
12. Colman, 64.
13. Markham, 64.
14. Markham, 53.
15. Anon. (1775), I, 229; Anon. (1588).
16. Hodgett, 16.
17. Hodgett, 21.
18. McNeil, 170.
19. Austin, 100.
20. Frere, 21.
21. Frere, 23.
22. Tusser, 25.
23. Anon. (1775), I, 229.
24. Thurley (1990), 20.
25. Frere, 47.
26. Frere, 51.
27. A.W., 6.
28. Simon (1959), 82.
29. Anon. (c. 1500).
30. Thurley (1993), 157.
31. Tusser, 3.
32. Harrison, 158; Murrell (1638), 11.
33. May, 194.
34. Gate.
35. Hodgett, 30; Austin, 78–80.
36. A.W., 27.
37. Herleian MS 276 in Furnivall (1868), 145.
38. Partridge (1585).
39. Furnivall, 8/97, 152/35.
40. Wilson, 303; Markham, 40–1.
41. BM Cott. MS Vesp. CXIV f. 105.
42. *HO* 42–3.
43. Hollingshead, III, 820.
44. *HO* 72.
45. Plat, 47.

Chapter 8 The Privy Kitchen

1. *HO* 158.
2. Thurley (1990), 21.
3. Markham, 52.
4. Dawson, I., 27.
5. A.W., 10.
6. Hodgett.
7. Hodgett, 14.
8. Hodgett, 15.
9. Hodgett, 13.
10. Dawson, II, 57.
11. Hodgett, 19.
12. Hodgett, 19.
13. Boorde, 274–5.
14. Hodgett, 20.
15. Boorde, 263; Hieatt and Butler, 62; Brears (1987), 172–4.
16. Hodgett, 20.
17. Austin, 79; Furnivall (1868), 103; Boorde, 270.
18. Furnivall (1868), 49; *HO* 430.
19. Jacques de Longuydon, Voeux de Paon, New York, Pierpont Morgan Library , Glazier, 24, f. 52.
20. Austin, 79.
21. Dawson, I., 7.
22. Hodgett, 18.
23. Hodgett, 18.
24. Nicholas, 83, 26/10/1536.
25. A.W., 25.
26. Hieatt and Butler, 119.
27. Boorde, 267; Hodgett, 24.
28. Strutt, II, 103.
29. *C SP Ven*, II, 918.
30. A.W., 31.
31. Dawson, II, 19.
32. *IKH* 76; Dawson II, 26; Brears (1993), 136.
33. Seager, 42.
34. Tusser, 256.

Chapter 9 Preparing for Dinner

1. *HO* 232, 71–2.
2. Cogan, 27.
3. *L&P 1541*, 503 (6); *1544*, I, 23.
4. See Simon (1959) 37–41, for a description of wines of the period.
5. Anon. (c.1500), f. 2.
6. *HO* 76.
7. Anon. (1508); Partridge (1585).
8. *L&P 1542*, II, 1251 (24); *HO* 233–4, 77.
9. *HO* 78.
10. *HO* 83.
11. *HO* 291, 196.
12. *L&P 1545*, I, 848.
13. Simpkinson, app. lx, iii (1633–4).
14. *HO* 83.

Chapter 10 Serving the King

1. *HO* 48.
2. *HO* 36, 42.
3. *HO* 36.
4. *HO* 192.
5. *HO* 113, 84; *IKH* 1143 et seq., 1747 et seq.
6. *IKH* 1616 et seq., 1553 et seq., 1418 et seq., 1468.
7. *HO* 84.
8. *IKH* 1502–4.
9. *IKH* 1323 et seq.
10. *IKH* 1678 et seq.
11. *IKH* 1505 et seq, 17218 et seq.
12. *IKH* 1928; *HO* 118, 115.
13. *IKH* 1766 et seq.
14. Anon. (c.1500).
15. *HO* 118, 114.
16. *HO* 152.
17. *IKH* 11198; Anon. (c. 1500).

18. *IKH* 1657 et seq.
19. *IKH* 1661.
20. *HO* 75.
21. *IKH* 1035.
22. *HO* 154, 109.
23. *IKH* 1927.
24. Furnivall, 272, 230–1, 358; *OED*, 'voider'.
25. *IKH* 1683–4, 1235, 1248.
26. E.G. *IKH* 11853 et seq, 17194 et seq, 11865–7.
27. *HO* 119.
28. *HO* 153.

Chapter 11 Dining in Chamber and Hall

1. *HO* 171.
2. *HO* 171–2.
3. Knell.
4. *HO* 83–4.
5. Furnivall.
6. Winchester, 146.
7. *IKH* 17619.
8. Furnivall, 22, 178, 255.
9. Furnivall, 178–9.
10. Furnivall, 157.
11. Furnivall, 22.
12. Furnivall, 279–80.
13. Brears (1987) 28, 76; (Hutton 1998), 16.
14. Adams, J., 19–20.
15. Adams, J., 19–20; *HO* 83–4.
16. Bread trenchers do not appear to have been made for the court in the 1540s, the only trenchers provenanced to this date being the wooden examples recovered from the *Mary Rose* (Barkeley, xlv; *HO* 72).
17. Barkeley, xlvii, xlvi.
18. *HO* 195, 78.
19. Barkeley, xxxvi.
20. Barkeley, xxxvii, xxxv.

ACKNOWLEDGEMENTS

I would like to thank the staff of Hampton Court Palace, especially Mr Dennis McGuinnes, Dylan Hammond, Anne Fletcher, Caroline Allington, Laura Cappellaro and Andrea Selley, together with all those who have warded and cleaned the kitchens during the Christmas events since 1991. Without their very positive assistance, it would have been impossible to have achieved such considerable success. Along with everyone interested in the history of the Tudor court, I also owe an enormous debt of gratitude to Dr David Starkey and Dr Simon Thurley, whose publications, of the highest scholarly excellence, have rendered so much primary evidence readily available for study. It should be stressed, however, that all views expressed in this book are entirely my own responsibility, having had no input from the curatorial staff of Historic Royal Palaces or elsewhere.

The practical operation of the kitchens has placed demands on all the historical interpreters who have worked here as Tudor cooks at the Christmas events. In addition to researching and making their own clothing, they have worked long days, frequently at sub-zero temperatures, chopping, pounding, turning spits, while still keeping up a constant flow of good-humoured, informative conversation with thousands of visitors. Then came the masses of washing and scouring of everything before retiring, exhausted, to their spartan garrets, just like their Tudor predecessors. For all this, and their friendship, I take the greatest pleasure in thanking the whole team: Marc Meltonville, Kane Allen, Lawrence Beckett, Andrew Butler, David Cadle, Barry Carter, Andrew Crombie, Richard Fitch, Robert Hoare, Marc Hawtree, John Hollingworth, Richard Jeale, Robin Mitchiner, Gary Smedley and Adrian Warrell.

Peter Brears
Leeds, 1999

GENERAL INDEX

NB The Definition of each unusual word is given where it first appears in the text

RECIPE INDEX